Back to Basics

Back to Basics

ARTHUR DALEY'S
ANATOMY OF BRITAIN

as told by
Andrew Nickolds

HEINEMANN : LONDON

First published in Great Britain in 1994
by William Heinemann Ltd
an imprint of Reed Consumer Books Ltd
Michelin House, 81 Fulham Road, London SW3 6RB
and Auckland, Melbourne and Singapore

Copyright © Andrew Nickolds 1994
The author has asserted his moral rights

A CIP catalogue record of this book
is available at the British Library
ISBN 0 434 00021 3

Typeset by Falcon Graphic Art Ltd
Wallington, Surrey
Printed and bound in Great Britain
by Mackays of Chatham plc, Chatham, Kent

THE BODYWORK

INTRODUCTION
What is Occurring?

Readers of discernment (by which I mean those of you who have handed over the folding stuff and are curling up with this book in the comfort of your lounge, rather than the inconsiderate browsing riff-raff who are cracking the spine, smudging the pages with greasy fingers and generally leaving it in an unfit state for the serious customer, WHAT DO YOU EXPECT FOR £9.99 – A TEST DRIVE ROUND THE BLOCK?) will recall that I very nearly got a result with my autobiography, *Straight Up*.

'What do you mean *nearly*, Arthur?' I hear you ask. 'Didn't *Straight Up* change lives, bring comfort to the afflicted and some serious relief to the publisher's balance-of-trade situation ... in short, do the business?' All this and more. But I must confess to a tinge of regret that inexplicably – and this is still the subject of scandalised gossip among the literary mob up at the Harpo Club – I was left off the short list for *all* of last year's book prizes. Nary a sniff from the Booker or the Whitbread ... and not even the courtesy of an acknowledgement from Betty Trask or Somerset Maugham – so much for marking letters 'Personal'!

I was consoling myself with the thought that Richard Burton had never won an Oscar, which naturally led on to consoling myself with a catering-size vodka and slimline (hereafter referred to as VAT) down the Winchester, when I happened to glimpse in my copy of *Competitors' Journal* news of another annual gong for the leading lights of Eng. Lit. Something told me that the NCR (National Cash Register) Award and I were destined to make beautiful music together.

But how to get the Daley moniker on its plinth? Now, I have to admit I wasn't planning on the Winchester as the seat of my inspiration. An eighteen-carat watering hole and safe haven for some of Fulham's finest denizenry, no question, but when it comes to matters bookish they're a lot happier with the runners and riders in the 2000 Guineas than they are with *2000 Leagues Under the Sea*.

Take Dave, for instance. As minehost he has no equal, the top man. Name one other who'll cash a forest of cheques at half a minute past four on a Friday afternoon? But when it comes to using the old grey matter, Dave is hardly *bacardi cum laudanum*. Reading a wallpaper book at Texas Homecare is about his lot. Even then his lips move.

And yet. As I pondered, something occurred that could have come from the fertile imagination of my late namesake, Arthur Kunstler. ' 'Ere,' Dave pipes up, 'I reckon I've got an idea for your next book. I've just been watching this programme where this English couple ups and offs to France, buys a crumbling house and gets into lots of scrapes with characters straight out of *'Allo 'Allo.'*

'They may actually be in *'Allo 'Allo*, Dave,' I replied, choosing my words carefully. On account of space and doing my bit for the environment the Daley Video Palace has creatively edited many a Hollywood blockbuster so that several fit snugly on one tape –

and you don't even see the join. However, it has created in Dave a lasting and worrying sense of visual disorientation. He once asked me if there was a sequel to *The Magnificent Seven City Slickers*.

'No, listen,' went on my Sanyo Panzer. 'Apparently it's based on the real adventures of this geezer and his book has been a bestseller for about forty years. Why don't you try something like that?'

'Hardly,' I said. 'You're forgetting 'er indoors. She gets seasick once we leave the 071 phone area. Gawd knows what would happen if I tried to ship her to the land of boules and baguettes.'

My boy came in in time to hear this last bit. 'You'll just have to do it from home, Arthur,' he said. 'Call it *A Year in Parson's Green*. You'll put SW6 on the map, the shops'll stay open another half-hour to cope with the tourist influx and next thing you know you'll have this lot calling round.' And he plonks down on the bar a copy of *Hello!* magazine, which specialises in informal studies of the *haute del monte* relaxing on their patios.

'That's not a bad idea at that,' I mused. 'The mountain coming to Mohammed kind of thing. I'd better make sure 'er is up that day. And I'll lay in a supply of Odor-Eaters.'

'I was joking,' said the boy, a smirk spreading over his boat.

'Terrible,' said Dave.

'Thank you, Dave,' I said. 'There's a starving reading public out there, desperate for crumbs dropping from my pen. And it's still on the launching pad! This is no laughing matter.'

'No, *this* is terrible,' said Dave. And he points to a picture in the magazine of Princess Di at Thorpe Park, frolicking in the Staines surf with the little princes, Wills and Squidgey or whatever his name is.

'I mean, what kind of world is it, Arthur,' continued Dave, warming to his theme, 'when your Royalty is up for wet T-shirt contests? Not to mention only having the kids at weekends? When we was young you didn't see the Queen Mum on a Big Wheel, or Prince Philip ringing the bell with an 'ammer. What's happening, Arthur? Everything seems to be changing. You don't even see the monkey puzzle trees you used to.'

It was almost a magic moment. You could have knocked me down with a proverbial. Dave had given me my idea! And it ain't just him who's going around like an extra in a zombie movie – nobody in the country today's got a clue either. When *Straight Up* walked off the shelves people knew what it was all about. Britain was a steady ship – Maggie was at the helm and all was right with the world. Premier League businessmen were wheeling and dealing with the best of 'em, purloining a fair share for Britain of whatever nice little earner happened to come sauntering by. The last dying twitches of the socialist menace – water, gas, National Theatre – were being sold off to ordinary punters (with ordinary-sounding names – that was the secret of multiple applications).

But now look. We've had businesses collapsing faster than 1960s tower blocks, miners marching in High Street Ken and the greatest leader since Winnie being seen off by a bunch of nerd-do-wells who can't even remember which off-licence they've been into the night before. Not to mention captains of industry only being allowed out of jug because they're suffering from Alzheimer's Disease ... and then forgetting they've got it. Britain in the 1990s is well out of order, I think you have to concur.

'Dave,' I said, 'you've only given me the subject for my next tome.'

'What's that, Arthur?'

'What's what, Dave,' I replied triumphantly.

'What?' asked a nonplussed Dave. Ah, the fine Lambrusco of conversation you get in the Winchester!

'*What's* what – I intend to put everybody straight on what is occurring in this land of ours. I'm going to write an A-to-Z for the hapless Brit currently lost in a mailroom of uncertainty. How to find the level playing field on top of the moral high ground. After finishing this the people'll never want to open another book again.'

'There'll be a large one waiting here when

you've finished, Arthur,' said Dave, a Greyfriars Bobby among men.

That seems like only a week ago. As it happens it was slightly less, publishers' deadlines and Notices of Distraint being what they are. It's been a bit like doing a marathon, without a tinfoil suit in sight. But I'm quietly confident that my labours have been worth it. You hold in your hand nothing less than a complete in-depth company report on Great Britain plc that makes the Doomsday Book look like a take-away menu from the Fulham Golden Palace.

Read on, Macduff!

Arthur Daley

THE MONARCHY

Here's one for you: what more than anything else sets Blighty apart from other countries? The answer's our Royal Family. ER indoors. Third World places like Holland name car ferries after their monarchs, and they can be seen bicycling round the red light districts and drinking oranjeboom with the rest of the hoypaloy. And in Spain King Don Juan did a Boris Yeltsin and threw himself in front of tanks in the name of liberty. Not very seemly, is it? I mean, can you see any of our lot disporting themselves like that? Apart from Princess Diana, bless her, cannoning into a drinks cabinet in one of her 100-yard sprints to the fridge. Talk about *It's a Royal Knock-Out*!

No, the great and admirable quality of the House of Windsor is their cool, aloof, regal behaviour. The next great thing about them is their talent for pulling in top dollar for said performance. Now to understand why HM has been so adept at the old financial ducking and diving you have to go back to history. Back through the mists of time to her ancestors, because by having a butcher's at them you see how all their hard graft has paid off for the later generations.

England didn't always have one monarch, you know. In the olden days of yore there were kings for dogs. It was a bit like the telly is now: you think there's one ITV, but it's made up of lots of smaller ITVs in the regions – Home Counties, South coast, Jocko land, all over. So you've got your King of Tyne Tees with his manor and he's the gaffer and has the final say about what time *Home and Away* goes out. Though Australia hadn't been discovered then, of course.

As one of these kings increased his credit worthiness by diversifying his portfolio – salt tax here, spot of pillage there – he saw his collecting agents or minders right and rewarded them with a share of the plunder . . . just like ITV again come to think of it, with their Golden Handcuffs share options system for your Melvyn Braggs and Roland Rats. I've tried to explain this noble historic tradition in his calling to my own boy, but he still insists on being paid in readies.

Now in them days without the ponies or Lloyds to flutter your ducats away on, you had to buy land – or, if you were temporarily strapped for cash, seize it. So the minders were all knighted and put up decent gaffs of their own, in which they kindly stored all the worldly goods and produce of the local peasantry, because with about fifteen of them and a donkey in one room space was at a bit of a premium. So next time you and the trouble take the kids for a day out at Alton Towers, keep in mind that a castle is basically a lock-up with turrets on – and that's a genuine historical snippet right out of the horse's mouth, straight up!

The other thing about these kings was, they all had dodgy names: Eric, Nogbad the Bad, Ethelred (also known as 'Duracell' in court circles on account of his being Unready). Then Debretts came along and decreed that there ought to be just one king, called something suitable that commanded instant trust and respect. What else but ARTHUR!

After those carefree and alison days of jousting and pulling the sword out of the stone and bungee-jumping off bouncy castles, not for the last time Merry England was caught napping by Europe in the shape of William the Conqueror – as he became after winning a bank holiday battle on the beach at Hastings.

But I'll say this for him: he had an eye for business, unlike Harold who just had an eye. Not only did King Bill produce the first telephone directory, he saw the tax advantages of planting trees when he knocked up the New Forest, the fruits of which society figureheads like Terry Wogan, Shirley Tesco and Pink Floyd are enjoying to this day.

We fast-forward a bit now to Liz the First, a half-timbered version of Lady Thatcher – and here's another bit of historical hallucination, courtesy of the Daley archives: round the Court, up the Tower and down Annabel's, Queen Liz was known as Olive Oil, due to her virginal nature. But she was no mug when it came to seeing pastures new in different hemispheres, realising that the Great Caravan Routes of the East meant more than just the A13 to Southend. So she sent off her boys, Walter Raleigh – who invented the bicycle and brought back the first duty-free fags – and Charlie Drake, to have a bit of a shoofti.

The Spanish are well peeved by this, having a bit of a taste for foreign business themselves, so they sent their Armada across to have a word. Well, we're laughing because the bull-fighting brethren have always been bit suspect away from their own turf – dodgy temperament, late tackles, that sort of thing – so they bottle it. Home win. What's more we're soon bestowing on them the fruits of *our* civilisation: proper drinking water, *Eldorado*, planeloads of True Brits singing The Birdy Song.

And ever since, the monarchy has been a dab hand at the old import/export game, despatching the sprogs round the world to keep associated royal families up to strength. Meanwhile we've let William of Orange, Mary Queen of Scots, Phil the Greek and Princess Michael of Kent take up citizenship. It's like breeding a racehorse: you've got to mix and match, a bit of fresh blood to rev up the old blue genes. But not just anyone, either. Getting a parking space on the balcony at Buck House makes the *Krypton Factor* look like *Mastermind* and vice versa, if you know what I mean.

A commoner embarking on life as a Windsor needs that delicate balance of grace, character and knock-out dress sense that will enable them to shoot the sherbet with ambassadors, heads of state and Barbra Streisand whilst at the same time keeping the odd yawn at bay when the whole family put on their kilts and start playing charades on Christmas Day. Such a person is one in a million.

But what do they do when they acquire a treasure like Fergie? No sooner has she put out for a new set of luggage for all them trips and got the double glazing installed in her palatial new stockbroker belt home than she's given the door. The Royal 'E'. Back on the rock-and-roll.

If you ask me, one of the wheels seems to have come off the gilt carriage of late: Royal family rows, fish-bones in the smoked salmon fillets, Prince Charles thinking he's been flushed down the karzy . . . worst of all, the Queen's in serious danger of sending her-self letters headed OHMS and having to write a gregory for the tax man!

It's as obvious as the nose on the face of Jim

*The Royals demonstrating that when it comes
to handing out sound financial advice,
they Know A Man Who Does.*

de Bergerac that what's needed here is some sound financial advice. And without wanting to be seen as a bit of a Les Majesty, I reckon I'm just the loyal subject to provide it . . . but if it's all right with you Ma'am, I'll keep the shoes and socks on.

As it happens this isn't the first time I've been in touch with her about the enterprise culture. Let Dave take up the story:

'You've done what, Arthur?'

'Written to Her Maj requesting a Royal Warrant for my new business, on account of it being a get-up-and-go venture that provides happiness and relief throughout SW6 at no cost to your punter and only an extra thirty pence if you inhabit the bandit country past Fulham Broadway.'

'You've asked the Queen for a warrant for your pizza delivery service?'

'Why not? It's all very well lavishing the grace and favour on saddle makers and titfer merchants up West, but what about the thrusting entrepreneur hacking his way through the jungle of the market-place?'

'Who's that, then?' asked Dave, a sentence behind as usual.

'And anyway, do you think Harrods started life as an Aladdin's Cave fit only for the likes of Joan Collins? No, back when Knightsbridge was a village,

Harrods was your corner shop. In you'd pop for a pint of milk and a couple of toilet rolls. You know, open all hours. Next thing you know Dozey and Mickey Fayed's ancestors have got videos for rent and are flogging papers. It's all about service, Dave – seeing what people want before they ask for it, having a deep pan Hawaiian with extra cheese on the doorstep just as the dog is lifted. I've seen the future, Dave, and there's a lot of pepperoni on it.'

I didn't hear back. Nevertheless, I'm quite prepared to do my loyal bit to help restore the monarchy to the position where it rightfully belongs, viz. Chairman of the Board. Her so-called advisers reckon it'll help the Sov rake in a few sovs by opening up selected corridors of Buck House to the punters.

Well I have to tell you I'm distinctly underwhelmed. Eight quid? That wouldn't get you a seat in the Gents at Wembley! What's wrong with rushing the Yanks a pony, giving them free access and turning a blind eye when they nick the Imperial Leather from the bathrooms? And forget all that 'Fid. Def.' cobblers on the coinage: 'Maximise One's Assets' should be the slogan going round the royal boat. Princess Margaret has as much right to a bit of appearance money for opening a new Kwiksave as Cilla Black.

I'll go further. What is it that best sums up Christmas, apart from turkey, brandy butter, dodging 'er indoors and the mistletoe and *The Great Escape* on the box? The Queen's Christmas Message, of course. A captive audience of millions with disposable income burning a hole in their pockets (assuming they haven't spent it already at the January sales the previous autumn). We know you like to show us your home movies of happy Commonwealth members bringing on a downpour in their grass skirts, Ma'am, but haven't you heard of product placement?

I've roughed out a few ideas for a more suitable message, based on my years of TV experience making ads for my used motor emporium – for those of you not lucky enough to have caught them because you were in bed, they went out in the Thames Television area (Dave says that's the reason they lost their franchise, but he can be a bitter man) and featured A. Daley (Prop.) in a series of humorous and dare-devil stunts like coming down on a parachute while giving my opening hours on Bank Holiday and timing the landing to perfection (see page 18 ... though I can confess now to all you tricks-of-the-trade buffs that I never went higher than three feet in a studio in Wandsworth).

So when Her Majesty's favourite film-maker Dickie Attenborough is off making 'Chaplin 2 – The Holborn Empire Strikes Back' or some such, I shall be in like flynn with the following script:

[*We see the Queen in her boudoir, pouring herself a cup of coffee from a gold pot then shaking a handful of beans in the royal mitt. She parks herself on an ormulu chair, turns to the camera and says:*]

Mmm – good coffee. Oh, hello! Well, what a year and no mistake! We thought all our troubles were behind us and blow us if Windsor Castle doesn't go and burn down. Doesn't that put the tin hat on it? Luckily we were covered by Legal and General, who don't make a drama out of a crisis. [FLASH UP PHONE NUMBER FOR PROSPECTUS]

So what have we been up to over the past twelve months? As usual, we've derived great warmth and comfort meeting our subjects the length and breadth of the country, thanks to the Royal Train. [FLASH UP PICTURE] Available at selected times for weddings, knees-ups and race meetings. Contains a fully-licensed buffet serving hot and cold snacks and your choice of fine wines. For that special occasion, ask for the Royal Bedchamber, with two-berth four-poster bed and minibar. [FLASH UP TARIFFS] Makes the going easy – and the coming back!

We have been pleased to visit our many grand-children, during their weekends with the parent on our side, and have been most impressed with the many improvements that have been made to the family homes. [FLASH UP PICTURE OF ANDY AND FERGIE'S GAFF, AKA 'SOUTH YORK'] Here for example, just off Junction 6 on the M4, you can stop and for only £5.99 try the Unique 'Surf and Turf' experience – a succulent prime cut of beef from the Royal herd

and a generous Dublin Bay Prawn, caught on the
Royal Yacht *Britannia* itself. Keep the kids amused
at the antics of Clown Prince Edward! Ample free
parking . . .

And so on. A couple of these, Ma'am, and I think
we're talking Annus Big Ackers-ilis!

HER MAJESTY'S GOVERNMENT

The smack of firm leadership, that's what the country's lacked ever since the greatest Englishwoman since Boderek sank beneath the waves, with her Trident Missile in one hand and an handbag the size of an electricity junction box in the other. And what's she left us with? A Cabinet that everyone can see has got less fibre than a fun-size box of Kelloggs. Talk about scandals – I don't remember anything like it since Ruby Keeler kicked her legs in the air in the 1960s and brought down Supermac and the golden era of 'You've never had it so good'.

I certainly never hadn't: cast your mind back to those exciting days of the Mini – the car that is, not the skirt. (Even when London was wall-to-wall dolly birds, 'er indoors was never much of a one for getting her knees brown, if you catch my drift. And she thought 'Kinky Boots' was when the chemist's in the Fulham Road started selling Soap-on-a-Rope). How did the poet put it? 'Bliss was it that dawn to be alive, but to be in the motor trade – that was the business!' Everybody had money burning a hole in their hipster pockets, they wanted to be mobile, and my forecourt was alive of a Saturday morning with worshippers at the shrine of Alec of Issigonis. If you bought a mini-moke with the roof permanently down I'd throw in a free dachshund. Goodbye Genevieve, hello The Italian Job.

Then Harold Wilson came along and spoilt everything. The sun went in and suddenly it was all naff plastic raincoats, BBC2 and the disposable pound in your pocket being worth ten bob. Everybody went back to travelling on red buses. And as for manners, they went right out of the window. It seemed an upright citizen couldn't even take a stroll down the King's Road in a smart camel coat without being jeered at by long-haired layabouts in a psychologically-painted Volkswagen.

And unless I'm very much mistaken, that Dark Age is about to sweep over us again if we're not careful. I'm ashamed to say that the rot was started by our local MP, Mavis Dellor (I've changed his name and orientation seeing as he's now paid his debt to society after appearing on TV with Terry Wogan). I'd had several promising discussions with Mavis, when he was appointed Minister of Fun and as such in charge of the National Lottery. This was in my capacity as a leading campaigner for such a sensible depository for people's disposable income, since in my view it was more overdue than Ronnie

Biggs's library books. I even offered the Minister the services of a secure lock-up for the purposes of printing the tickets, stashing the stake money, etc. And then what happens? His own number comes up when he's caught in flagrant dereliction giving some starlet's extremities a good seeing-to. And worse still – not only was the silly boy playing away, but in a *Chelsea home strip!!* I hold my hand up. What can you do?

Of course, Mavis didn't resign, and it was well past drinking-up time when Black Rod came knocking on the door of Parliament with his mace and had him carried out by his bulldogs. And this is what brings me to the crunch of my argument. Nowadays nobody does the decent thing, however bang they're caught to rights. The only place you'll see the decanter of scotch and the loaded revolver in the library drawer now is in an episode of Mrs Marple. And while I think about it – AA men saluting, standing still for the National Anthem at the end of the pictures and giving up the blue packet of salt in your crisps to a lady have all turned their toes up too. Chivalry's not just dead, it's starting to hum.

I blame the Classless Society. Did John Major go blue at Eton? Has he got the stiff upper lip of your traditional British toff? Did he play fives or party sixes for his house, or get touched up by the KGB at Cambridge or serve with distinction in the Bengal Lancers? No. Instead he failed his bus conductor's exam. Oxford? He couldn't find Oxford Circus. He must have been to see *The Dirty Dozen* a good few times when there wasn't a matinee at the circus though, because no sooner had he taken over the wheel of the Good Ship Great Britain than he packed the bridge with an assortment of riff-raff and truth economists whose family mottoes were Latin for 'Not Me, Guv' and 'I'm All Right, Jack', or Julius as it was then.

There've been Ministers claiming child benefit for their little indiscretions up Hackney way, getting ladies of the night evicted from their basements at the expense of the hard-pressed taxpayer (that's you) even stories about Ministers getting into bed with footballers! (Chelsea again, as like as not.) Any Old Irons can get their snouts in the trough these days it seems, and when they've got bored with being one of the Movers in the Commons, they get kicked upstairs to join the Shakers in the Lords. And with the peerage come some perks of course: a nice tax-free per diem, subsidised grub and a hot water bottle for your plates.

Meanwhile the country goes to rack and ruin. So I say ENOUGH IS ENOUGH. It's time for our elected leaders who've been living off the fat of the land for too long to take their hands out of the till and put them where their mouths are. If they want to get into bed with anyone, let it be with Arthur Daley plc! It so happens that I have a myriad variety of off-the-peg companies in my bailiwick, the boards of which would all benefit from the addition of a Cabinet Minister, even a shop-soiled one.

Let's take just one at random: Arthur Daley Landscape Gardening Ltd. I think it was the Duke of Westminster who said, 'An Englishman's home is his castle'. His Lordship never spaketh a truer word. Whether it's some legoland duplex down Canary Wharf or one of them plush palaces with the gravel drive in Weybridge, we English take considerable jam tart from the repose of our gaffs. Artex, manicured lawns, crazy paving, ornamental ponds and gnomes with fishing rods are just some of the cogs in the barometer of national taste, ingredients for a recipe that add up to a feast of extramural delights that we have fed our minces on, century in, century out. It seemed only natural that a patriot like myself should undertake the social work of trying to enhance the gardens of England. Not to mention the eight tons of pieces of Berlin Wall I'm still trying to find good homes for.

But for every vista crying out for a limpid rock pool and waterfall with goldfish leaping up it, there's some interfering council jobsworth belly-aching about planning permission and pointing out by-laws that say you can't even sort bones on Whit Monday, let alone move a JVC in. Well, this is where my ex-Cabinet Ministers ride into town, wearing their Daley Board of Directors hats. They'll know exactly what sweeteners to lay on for the pen-pushers, using the cutting-edge know-how that led to such export/import successes as arms to Iraq and coal to Newcastle. What's more, when the trade mission has done its work and the local plod has been issued with its new night-sticks (or whatever the quid pro quid turns out to be) I wouldn't mind betting that my boys even manage to get the bill for landscaping the pond picked up by the ratepayers. (That's you, again.)

Commerce should work hand-in-glove with government is what I'm saying, and none of that nonsense about trying to stick honest businessmen in jug merely for flogging metal tubes to the towel-heads. In the old days those lads from Dot Matrix would have been given a Duke of Edinburgh's Award, not a spell of residence at Her Majesty's Pleasure. Of course, industry is a four-wheeled drive up a two-way street, and Arthur Daley plc would expect something in return, a coconut for all this bounty. For every blue-chip directorship I hand out I'd want a seat on a Quango, right up there with the barbecue pot noodle as one of this century's diamond inventions.

Just like money makes the world go round, Quangos make you go round the world, on fact-finding freebies to investigate hydro-electric schemes in New Zealand that provide vital savvy-faire when it comes to planning pensioners' water meters in Hammersmith. There's usually a chauffeur-driven motor thrown in, and sometimes if you're a good boy a place on the local Police Authority or Hospital Trust (the word what reassures the punters that their kidneys are safe in your hands). Needless to say my boat would fit very nicely on one of these august bodies. And this brings me to my Big Idea, a wheeze which with one bound will free the Government from the shackles of contumely it currently vegemites in, and what's more will set the cash tills at Number 11 playing a chorus of 'Jingle Bells' all year round.

The Sincerest Form of Philately

When it became crystal that the National Lottery was a closed book of stubs as far as yours truly was concerned, what with the dibs being already earmarked for so-called artists who seem two Burnt Umbers short of a palate – like that sculptoress who copped a score of monkeys just for filling up her gaff with ready-mixed concrete instead of student nurses, and they say there's an housing shortage! – I put on my thinking trilby and, after five minutes, Europa!

At the bottom of the wardrobe, among the André Kostelanatz 78s and a bundle of personal missives tied up with a ribbon that to this day give off the effluvial waft of nostalgia – modesty permits me to reveal their contents, but if I say the names Dr Emil Savundra, Horace Bachelor and John Bloom, that should give you an idea – I found my old Stanley Gibbons stamp album. Now there was a man – not only a member of the immortal Bolton Wanderers forward line, but the inventor of the 'On Approval' cash-flow system, that turned this young shaver's barnet away from the groves of Academe to the higher slopes of Ackers.

What happened was, you'd get through the post a cellophane packet of stamps, showing exotic birds of paradise and great big triangular ones from Fiji of women with soup-plates in their bottom lips (that was before they joined the Commonwealth and we showed them how to use the knife and fork). So of course you stuck 'em straight into your album, or if you'd already got the packet took it to school and swapped it for a spud gun. It wasn't till you got home that you found you'd forgotten to read the ad properly, and you now owed Stan two and threepence. Result: Dad took his belt off and you learnt your first lesson from the Harvard Business School of Life: make the small print too hard to read.

Stan had cottoned on to an eternal verity about this island race: we've got *Exchange and Mart* coursing through our veins. Bus tickets, fag cards, hub-caps – every true son and heir of the late great John Bull is a collector. The Post Office, that dozy monolith that gives dyslexia a bad name – they read 'Gone Away' and think it says 'Try Again And Keep Knocking' – is only just waking up to this and has decided in its infinite to issue special stamps of kiddies' drawings not just at Christmas but all year round. They've even let Prince Charles have a crack at it with his etchings and all I can say is Gawd help us if his shaky finger's ever allowed to stray near The Button. Stick to turning out the monogrammed Hovis, old son.

Most likely you're a couple of blocks ahead of me now. All HMG has to do to rake in the rhino is forget about dodgy so-called earners like charging widows an arm and a leg every time they want to spend a penny, and bring out every week a new set of stamps, Limited Edish, in large denominators. The queue outside the front door of your sub post office will be longer than them for the Giro, Harrods sale and the Winchester at Happy Hour put together! And if it's of a national monument or treasure that'll bring a lump to the throat of all those expat Brits building dams in Kuala Lumpa or digging kibbutzes in the Holy Land, so much the better. Might I volunteer this as an artist's impression of the first issue?

The occasional printer's error, almost invisible to the naked eye, can nevertheless send an auctioneer's hammer rocketing through Sotherby's roof.

That's what I call a Commemorative Mug! Bung 'em in a presentation pack with a first-day cover and a solar-powered calculator, get the Royal Mint to print up the odd duff sheet with the cigar ash missing and you can kiss ta-ta to the National Debt.

THE CITIZEN'S CHARTER
The Arthur-ised Version

All of our recent Government supremos have had an endearing kink in their armour, something that adds a human touch to the footnotes of the yet-to-be-transcribed history of our people and puts us on a pedestal as an Ever Ready Derby among races. The late great Winnie shared my taste for a fine Monte Cristo cigar and kept a dead budgie in a cage. Maggie was famous for letting a motherly tear or two rust her ferrous metal exterior when she heard her boy Mark had been found alive and setting up a Malvern Water franchise in the Sahara Desert. Even Ted Heath managed to combine his two hobbies, by arranging for his brass band to play on the quayside at Chichester when he got back from sailing round the world single-handed.

But how is the future going to remember the present encumbrance at Number 10? What's the Big Idea that he's going to be indelibly associated with, like Garibaldi and the Hob-nob? Motorway cones. Would you believe it? But then again, in the immortal dying words of my old Dad Arthur Daley Snr, never put too much faith in a geezer who tucks his shirt into his pants. Not to mention leaves a Bermuda Triangle of bare leg showing between sock and trouser. Anyway, the country that gave birth to Caxton and such masterpieces of the scribe's art as Magna Carta, Hansard and the *Currant Bun* now finds itself at the mercy of the Citizen's Charter, the greatest threat to freedom and democracy since Hitler and that fat clown Musso who bungee-jumped off lamp-posts.

Now I've got nothing percy about Taking Things Back. If Marks and Sparks didn't operate their admirable and trusting policy of Monday morning refunds no questions asked, there would have been many weddings round my manor that wouldn't have had the benefit of the Daley presence, resplendent in off-the-peg snazzy whistle. And bunging a half-eaten box of Black Magic off to Rowntrees after sticking your thumb through the orange creams and getting a replacement box (plus your stake back) is all part of the traditional English Christmas. What's more it's the healthy rough-and-tumble of commerce, the bartering system that we gave to Germany and Eastern Europe just after the last conflict to help 'em rebuild their economies. But now it seems Whitehall bureaucracy has once more gone beresk after John 90, the puppet with the ginormous bins, got bored one winter's night with no bowling averages to write down in his notebook and decided to bash out a few new dos and don'ts under the heading of 'The

Customer Is Always Right' – that pony old chestnut which has got about as much grip on reality as when that weather bloke in the day-glo sports jacket told us 'There won't be a hurricane' and next thing my lad's pulling a Metro out of a tree by its exhaust pipe.

The thought of disgruntled punters banging on the door of the lock-up at all hours, waving their Charters and demanding satisfaction of the readies variety gave me the screaming abdabs, so I decided to have a butcher's at the enemy on the eve of battle so to speak, put on my dark glasses and popped into Her Majesty's Stationery Office. The Queen must have already tooled herself up with Basildon Bond for that day, because I was allowed to browse uninterrupted.

What I read filled me with the kind of foreboding you get when a plod's helmet is silhouetted in the frosted glass of your front door. So in a spirit of getting your retaliation in first as Vinny Jones might say, here are my point-by-point suggestions for fine-tuning the Charter and making it a document that not just the pampered few consumers but the average everyday Citizen in a sheepskin and Jag can take comfort and solace in . . .

*A dynamic Government Charter Committee seen
compiling a Cone Census. Yours Truly is on hand
as the statuesque Citizen's Representative,
advising on the privatisation of parking tickets
in the West London area and furnishing a list
of on-the-spot fine collectors whose
morals are above question (as Dave will verify).*

Raising the Standard

This is a bit of a red flag to a bull for any patriot like me who gets a lump to his throat whenever he hears a crowd and the band at Wembley bring the National Anthem to four different conclusions. I mean to say, raising the standard is what King Charles did against that early hunt saboteur Oliver Cromwell over the right to wear feathered hats. And all he got for his pains was the Pub Grub treatment: his head in a basket. But apparently what the Grey 'Un in Downing Street means by it is 'To make public services answer better to the wishes of their users, and to raise their quality overall – ambitions of mine ever since I was a local Councillor in Lambeth over 20 years ago'.

Twenty years ago! I don't know what it was like in Lambeth (apart from them eating their young) but in Fulham in them days it was all fields. Or at any rate parking spaces stretching over the hills as far as the human eye could see. But that was before the Great War broke out, between Tommy Atkins going about his lawful business in his motor, and the Huns and Visigoths in the shape of traffic wardens and towaway trucks on piecework. *This is the ugly mug of local government, which* pounces on its innocent citizenry, takes away its lifeblood (said motor) and costs you an arm and a leg to get it back – worse if you try to climb over the barbed wire. So if the Whiteshirts at the Town Hall really want to be user-friendlier, Phase One in *my* charter would be to close down all the pounds, and turn them back into the wide open spaces of used car emporia where the punter can graze and roam freely like the American buffalo and other endangered species.

Neighbourhood Watch

Your humble co-respondent was on the front row when the notion of community spirit was handed out, and I remember with a warm nostalgic glow straight out of the pages of Marge Proust those dark days when everybody queued to fill a bucket from the tap at the end of the road, or trooped down the station steps to huddle together sleeping on Underground platforms (I hear this last tradition still continues regarding the last train to Upminster on a Saturday night). But these days it seems everybody being in and out of each other's houses means you wake up to find a square patch of dust where your home entertainments centre formerly resided, while a couple of score changes hands down Brick

Lane market. Borrowing a bob for the gas meter is now the speciality of the ram-raiding brethren, who leave you with a hole in the wall, two hanging wires and nary a note saying Ta muchly.

Of course nobody feels more Tom-and-Dick about this moribund state of public morality than I, and I hereby extend the warm velvet glove of welcome to the Neighbourhood Watch Scheme, in fact I think it doesn't go far enough. I propose that each street should get together its own posse of public-minded citizens, who will be on the constant key viva or at least their surveillance cameras will (author can supply – genuine ex-Pakistani grocers). Not just for the obvious villains – tea-leaves, petermen, etc. – but also the following undesirables:

- Pairs of chubby geezers eating crisps and sitting in unmarked jamjars parked across the road from your gaff;

- Geezers with briefcases studying A-to-Zs (unless the briefcases are embossed with the word 'Littlewoods', 'Zetters' etc);

- Geezers with ID cards giving you a lot of old moody about being unemployed and just down from the North;

- Convoys of New Age Travellers (easily spotted from their advance party's accoutremons – cans of Strongbow and dogs on strings);

- Hippies with squeegees at traffic lights trying to clean your windscreen for a sov. There are official recognised bodies for that sort of thing;

- Carol singers.

I for one will not rest until the streets of Fulham are free from this riff-raff. Vigilantes is the watchword. Not to mention NIMMTY (Not In My Manor, Thank You).

Identifying Staff

This was an idea started by British Rail, who used to give all their engines names like Thomas the Tank Engine and James the Red Engine – it gave me considerable grief as a kiddie that there wasn't an Arthur the Shrewd Engine, but then as now, if your face doesn't fit . . . After it had been a hit on the telly thanks to that drummer with the big hooter, BR hit on the wheeze of giving their workforce names too, and now you can't get on the dog to any organisation without hearing some Essex lemon's voice giving it with 'Ilford Breakdown Service, Jump-Leads We Got 'Em, Sandra speaking, how can I help you?'

To be honest, this is a bit of a two-edged sword of Demosthenes (Kojak's brother, to the less educated). Daley's First Law of Politeness does indeed stress the personal touch, but to me there is no substitution for the firm handshake and the eye-to-eye contact which renders anything written down completely redundant. My word is my bond, as those tic-tac blokes in opera hats on the Stock Market floor used to shout at each other. After all, the name 'Arthur Daley Motors' is emblazoned above the unspoilt beach that is my forecourt, so why does the satisfied customer need to see it pinned to my lapel? If the wearing of badges should happen to be made compulsory, then a quick trip to a Photo-Me booth should work the oracle. After all, a picture is worth a thousand verbals.

Waiting Times

I'm absolutely Bing Crosby with the PM on this one: right down the middle. It's a scandal that senior citizens can be kept waiting for a new hip on a trolley in a hospital corridor until the proverbial cows' homecoming, while some pinstripe with more letters after his name than Audrey Murphy can blue the budget bringing down his handicap at Moor Park. The same goes for the so-called dental profession: I reckon 'er indoors has been waiting for a new set of hampsteads since before the decimal coinage. I suggested going private, but she's got into the habit of taking her meat and two veg via straw, so she couldn't hear me and I thought best leave it. Though I did call an Emergency Helpline at 44p per minute, and it cost me a Lady Godiver to hear them suggest that she used the inside of a biro tube, because they're washable.

I wasn't going to take this lying down so without much further ado I belled our local Ombudsperson. By one of those coincidences life can ambush you with, like the Cold Weather Allowance falling due on the very day the warm snap starts, he turned out to be a geezer I'd sold a motor to the previous month.

'How's she travelling, Mr O?' I asked. 'Sweet as a nut, I bet.'

'Perfectly nicely, thank you Mr . . . I don't think I caught your name [see above]. Except there's a bit of a draught where the radio you promised me ought to be.'

'Ah – that's because there's a waiting list,'

I said, then realised I'd have to think fast
if I wasn't going to be hoisted on my own
petardis.

'So when can I come and collect it?'

'Well now, you have to realise that the
world of accessories is a lot more complicated
than your medical profession – you can't just
stick a new ticker or kidney in and hope for
the best. This is a delicate and painstaking
operation. The climate has to be right, not
forgetting the appropriate humidity . . .'

'Just to install a radio?' he scoffed.

'The climate in *Taiwan*,' I said, as if to a
five-year-old child. 'According to my overseas
operatives the plane hasn't taken off yet. Talking of which, your gregory seems to be a little
behind schedule arriving at my local branch
of Coutts. Circling the runway, is it?'

'I was waiting for you to deliver your part
of the bargain.'

I had him. 'Come come, Mr O,' I said.
'Let me draw your attention to the section of
the Citizen's Charter marked "Redress Against
Government Agencies". I quote. "If a Crown
body is found to be falling below standards,
enforcement authorities can go to the courts
for a declaration of non-compliance, which
would be followed by immediate corrective
action".'

'But *I'm* the enforcement authority!' he

shouted, losing his rag by now a bit and audibly perspiring.

'Exactly,' I concluded. 'You've got yourself bang to rights. Have the dibs round here in cash by close of today's business and I won't tell teacher.'

I reckon I scored Perfect Sixes there on the old Charter Marks. That's what I call Giving Power Back to the Individual, right John?

Jargon,
The Doing Away–with Of

I offer this as a prime example:

I hereby guarantee that I waive all rights, moral, financial and any others under the terms of the Geneva/Fulham Convention having purchased this vehicle, and if I try and stir up any trouble vis-à-vis dodgy engine or parts falling off I am liable to incur the wrath of the Proprietor (Arthur Daley) in the shape of a fatwa against myself and my family, or at the very least lose my house.

Signed in my absence ....

LAW AND ORDER
Meet The Woodentops

Law and Order – the joist and floorboard upon which the front room of every civilised society is built – has got a touch of the Picassos: the old bill are in their blue period. Instead of pursuing a decent vendetta against villains like their job description recommends, they're either too busy queueing up to go on telly with Shaw Taylor, or harassing patriots and entrepreneurs, or in the case of Stoke Newington setting up a drug cash-and-carry to rival the prescription counter at Timothy Whites. The only nick they've ever heard of is Nick Ross.

Things have got highly out of order since Sir John Peel opened Scotland Yard for business back in Victorian times. Before him there was all sorts of aggro with highwaymen, footpads doing Bow Street runners and Margaret Lockwood sticking her musket in the boat of unsuspecting wayfarers on the A2, demanding their lucre or their life. Travelling by stage-coach was more traumatic than going Network South-East, not counting New Cross Gate when Millwall are playing at home. If the Peelers did happen to get a result it was down to Marble Arch for Judge Lionel Jeffries to don the black hanky. There was no call for prisons because if you happened to escape the drop then it was a one-groat one-way assisted passage Down Under without water, a dollop of sunblock or a stop by the duty-free. You've only got to look at Merv Hughes to see what that did to a man.

The only felons who did stir were debtors, who were banged up in South London which take my word for it is punishment enough. They put in the hours of community service by carving poles for sedan chairs and sewing silk purses out of sows' ears that were left over from hog roasts at evening meetings at Sandown Park. Just imagine that kind of short sharp shock happening to all them members of the fancy on the Lloyd's List! Mind you, bung 'em in a windowless dingly dell with no karzy for twenty-three hours a day and it'd just remind them of their prep schools. They'd be begging for more.

Anyway, by the reign of Good Queen Vic there was a perilous need for the boys in blue (or black, this being the era before colour). The law-abiding bourganvillea had well and truly got the hump about seeing their hard-earned disappearing over the horizon in a couple of saddle bags. So Sir John puts down his stirrup cup and invents the old bill, or the young bill as it was then. This fine bunch of men took a stiff truncheon to petty criminals like Oliver Twist, Eric

Sykes and Michael Fagan and ensured that London was a safe place for the great and good to do business and desport themselves with a pinch of Wills Best Snuff.

So what has gone wrong? Why now do we find members of the Met's Finest creating havoc and misery in the lives of model citizens like Sir Ernie Saunders and Roger Sealink whose only crime was to ensure a few bob came England's way? Fortunately the bench saw that Sir Ernie had copped Alka Seltzer's, ploughed the green fields of compassion and set the man free just in time to make a full recovery.

I need not relate to you, Dear Reader, the hassle I too have endured over the years at the leathery hands of the plod. All I have ever sought, stand on me, was to make an iota of profit and put back into my country a morsel of what I have taken out. And yet at every crossroads and lay-by in life's journey I have been beset by the needless and overbearing attentions of some demented rozzer with an attitude. Have they never heard of the phrase 'Strike while the iron's hot'? Opportunities must be grabbed, and if the lynx-eyed and mountain-goat-footed amongst the business community are to put Britain back on the map then this may occasionally entail tethering the motor on a double yellow – the puniest of infringements when set against the benefits of tipping the balance of trade onto a favourable incline and getting millions back to work, I think you'll agree.

But why, I hear you angrily demand, is this attack on your civil liberties occurring, Arthur? The answer is Performance Related Pay. Now I am the first person to champion the free market, the teachings of Adam Faith and the Seven Dwarves of Zurich, but this is very District Line chocolate machine – out of order. We've got Dixon of Plod Green haring round sticking clamps on motors stopped loyally at a red light, blagging people for next to no reason in order to qualify for a bit of bunce at the end of the month. Targets, that's the name of the caper these days. Time was you just turned into a pumpkin at midnight – now it's make ten collars by the witching hour and cop a microwave for a bonus. It's one thing to go in for Economy Seven on the electric – 'er indoors won't put the Hotpoint on or get the iron out to do my bits and bobs till just before dawn, all to save a few pennies (the Smalls Hours we call them chez Daley). Which is fair enough. But not when it comes to enforcing the law: old Peely must be proceeding in a circular direction in his grave!

After the Citizen's Charter, though, (see page 31) little Johnny Englander knows his rights and whether he's bang to 'em or not. You can't any longer finger a geezer for wearing a shiny tracksuit while driving a big motor weighed down with furry dice and other accessories in dubitable taste, however natural the justice of it may seem. So right now the bill's petty cash book is looking very iffy as everyone's suing them for the humbrage they've caused. If they were the Met plc it would be time to reinvest elsewhere.

But not into Group 4, you are probably thinking. Of course, they have run into a bit of flak and derision of late, but then all businesses hit patches of turbulence when they diversify. My Mr Blobby Egg-Cups for Ethiopia Aid Scheme comes to mind. Carting a hundredweight of ten pences and Green Shield stamps into Tesco's is a bit different to chauffeuring round the hardened criminal classes, though numerically they may be the same. All they lack is a bit of expertise. Down the Winchester there are several reformed characters who have done their time and paid their debt to society if nothing else. In my humble they'd be ideal for any private security firm involved in Government business. They'd be onto every trick and wile in the book. Rest assured, with the likes of Lenny the Ladder and Suitcase Murphy at the helm of a reinforced Transit there would be no question of prisoners doing a bunk and booking themselves a one-way Poundstretcher to Folkestone Docks. What's more they would act as role models for the green and impressionable at this intersection of their young lives between salvation or a lifetime of institutional cooking. It's just a walk across the street between lawmaking and lawbreaking.

Behind These Walls

These days the ungrateful not to mention unshaven Antipodeans won't even let in law-abiding Brits after putting them through a sheep dip, let alone our criminal classes – so offenders have to do their porridge at home. The trouble is prisons, like our football grounds (and the similarity doesn't end there), are all smack in the middle of town with no room for belt-loosening. Criminals breaking out of Pentonville in North London have only got a short stroll down to King's Cross station, kit themselves out at the Tie Rack and the Sock Shop, and they're away. Give it a year and they'll be perusing some à la carte French cuisine on Le Shuttle long before the sirens have gone off and the bloodhounds have even picked up the scent.

So in tomorrow's Britain the nicks are going to have to move. This presents an ideal opportunity for going Back to Basics – a partnership between Government and the private sector. Thanks to the Tories' heroic championing of our rights as individuals there are whole areas of the country that have never seen a train. Stick the prisons in hinterlands like Merseyside, Tyne and Wear and Harlow and there would be no chance of escape. Let them break out. After a couple of days spent roaming the countryside without seeing a living soul except the odd wild boar they'd be back knocking on the gate, in dire need of a hot bowl of gruel extract and asking about the last episode of *EastEnders*. Better still, stick all the prisons on those Scottish Alcatrazes full of puffins and nuclear waste. Or even the Isle of Man, where they still hang people for chicken abuse.

Moving the prisons like this would create a golden economic triangle. In a trice the construction industry up North would be rejuvenated. And why not sort out some sponsorship – why go to the trouble of producing unpopular prison grub when the inmates could live on a diet of quarter-pounders? I can see it now – McStrangeways. Naturally, each consignment would have to be screened at the gate, to check for hidden files or meat content, but a happy bunch of campers would be the outcome, daisy-fresh every morning, whistling and jingling their chains as they go to work breaking rocks for a much-needed bypass or motorway extension.

In other words, build a prison and the next thing you know you've got yourself an enterprise zone!

BANKING
AND THE MONEY MARKETS

If there's one thing that sums up our sad decline
from the lofty heights among the Premier League of
nations to the relegation zone of the Beazer Homes,
it's the parlous state of your average High Street
ham-shank. I can speak with some authority on this
subject, having been not only one of the celebrat-
ed Lloyd's Names in my time, but also a NatWest
Name, a Midland Name and a Barclays Name at
various stages of my cheque-card career. The fact
that these once-august bodies have seen fit to close
A. Daley Premier Business Accounts almost before
the ink was dry on the dotted is, I have to say, a chill-
ing metaphor for the lack of confidence afflicting this
benighted country.

In fact I wrote expressing these very epigrams to
this week's occupant of the manager's hot seat, some
brat just out of college where they'd taught him how
to shave and say No in ten different languages (this is
the bank that likes to say Yes, I might add). And how
did he reply, this flies-wings puller-offer whose feet
could barely touch the pedals of his company Sierra?
With the tersest of notes informing me that not only

could my overdraft *not* be extended until the weather picked up, but also that they were charging me £27.50 just for some Sharon to carry the letter down to the post-room once her cuticles had been buffed! Me, of all people – voted 'Man Most Likely To' three years running by the Fulham Chamber of Commerce! The alarm bells should have gone off when I saw that the letter started 'Dear Former Valued Customer'.

How different matters fiscal were when a gregory didn't take a fortnight to clear (while the interest is being siphoned off into the bank's Christmas Club fund) and the man behind the desk was a trusted family friend instead of a few chromosomes short of a human being. It goes without saying I'm referring to the 80s – the 1680s – when everybody walked round like something off the lid of the Quality Street tin, and the Old Lady of Threadneedle Street was exactly that, a dear in a bonnet who ran a corner shop in the city. What happened was, wealthy merchants would stop off to buy a few ounces of snuff and a packet of Rizlas before hailing a sedan chair to take 'em out to Epping Forest for a day's wild boar hunting, their version of squash. Of course these merchants didn't want their hard-earned sovs falling out of their breeches' pockets, so the Old Lady volunteered to look after the ackers till they came back hot and sweaty and brandishing a couple of trotters from the day's sport.

Now this senior citizen was no mug (it would

surprise me not at all to find out that she was an old *Daley* of Threadneedle Street) because what she did when the chaps were out yoiks-and-tally-hoing was pop round the Stock Exchange and stick the lot on some gilt-edged commodity like Rolls-Royce (or Rollf-Royfe as it was in them days, before the invention of false hampsteads when everybody spoke funny). Of course, there was the occasional spot of grief when a cargo-ship of oriental rugs sank off the Azores (like it says in the small print, your investment can go down as well as up), but the Old Lady had the foresight to lay off her bet with the geezer next door who ran the coffee shop, by the name of Lloyd.

Being a crafty Taff he soon realised that beverages were small beer compared to the rich pickings of the insurance market, and thus was born the mighty company of Lloyd's of London, whose workings have ever since been shrouded in secrecy (though you can see the lavs being flushed if you go and stand outside the building). All of a sudden though, history has started repeating itself: a couple of oil tankers run aground after their skippers have spent the evening knocking back the anti-freeze and the next thing you know, panic-stricken Lloyd's syndicate members find themselves completely boracic and start rushing like llemmings for the double-garage with lengths of rubber tubing. Which I need hardly tell you is very bad publicity for the motor trade.

So here if ever there was one is a case for Back to Basics: to restore the good name of banking, and resuscitate those happy carefree days when the streets were paved with Gold Cards, the Black Horse tossed its mane in friendly greeting, and smiling managers said, 'That'll do nicely' to whatever far-sighted proposition you cared to stick in their parking-space. Remember that telly ad where the yuppie comes in and outlines his requisites to the men in grey whistles behind the desk? 'Unlimited free credit, sir? No probs. Bit of a sub to be going on with? My pleasure – Sharon, leave your nails alone, open up the till and give our pony-tailed friend here a couple of monkeys, clean notes only if you'll be so good.'

Servility costs nothing, I think you'll agree, and what's more it needs to be like that again. Banks seem to have forgotten that just like the Old Lady all those egons ago, it's *your* money they've got stashed away in those holes in the wall and not theirs to squander on flash foyers made out of the finest marble. I knew exactly how old Elgin must have felt when I read about that – it's mine, give it back! Nor will I be fobbed off any more with that glossy bumf which comes through the letter-box every morning, what you find piled up like a snowdrift if you've been away on business for the weekend and 'er indoors has decided on a bit of a lie-in. You know the sort of thing: telling me I've probably already won fifty grand, the Safari holiday of a lifetime and mortgage relief for life for my in-laws' dependants . . . and all I have to do to claim my prizes is add another credit card to my already groaning wallet – there's more plastic in there than in Michael Jackson. These come-ons are a grievous insult to the intelligence: anyone with a slide rule and a quarter of an hour to spare will twig as I did that every mention of 'Daley', 'the Daley household', etc. was a fraction of a centimetre above the rest of the letter – yet another con perpetuated on the Great British Public, just like those geezers in the linens who dole out the 'Spot the Ball' largesse after picking their own spot to put it (a blot on our sporting escutcheon of which you may not previously have been fully cognitive).

DALEY DIRECT BANKING on the other hand is a bony fido operation which will take tender loving care of your dibs and cut out the middle-men at the bank and such attendant humiliations as them holding up fifty-notes to the light to check if they're kosher. All a punter subscribing to this cutting-edge financial and insurance package has to do is get on the trumpet to my highly trained and polite staff. He'll note down what jack-and-jills they want paying, wait till the red ones and/or threats of bumbailiffs arrive – allowing 'em to cop for a chunk of interest – and Robert's your father's brother!

As a further passport to financial comfort every

client will be issued with a handsome Arthur Daley Smart Card (see illustration) welcome in filling stations, fast food parlours and wherever the Daley name is legion. They will also be fully covered against the vagrancies that affect the insurance market – house burning down, earthquakes, Chelsea being relegated, etc. That's it, in a dry roast nutshell. No frills, no junk mail, no £27.50 letters.

Your entree to the top tables of Society. This Smart Card is unlike any other in being made of specially treated tungsten steel, allowing it to do duty as a door-opener in the event of the owner being inadvertently locked out of his gaff. It will also withstand the efforts of bolshie waiters to cut it up in front of the owner and his dining companions, in a financial-embarrassment-after-a-good-blow-out scenario situation..

And all it costs to hop under this warm blanket of security? A mere lump sum, calculated according to means and a painless check on your credit rating from my staff. Said lump will then be wisely invested in blue-chip securities by yours truly, and five will get you ten (to coin a phrase) that the interest accruing will more than cover your everyday banking needs, from standing orders to charitable donations, many of which as my tax advice staff will point out can be offset as a business expense. Become a Daley's Name and you may never want to leave the house again, particularly if availing yourself of my Home Shopping Network (see page 178).

Like it says in the pools, dividends are expected to be good!

MAKERS OF BRITAIN
IN THE 20th CENTURY

You have to admit, we live in a Something-For-Nothing society. This sad fact came home to me the other day in no uncertains when I was standing at the checkout in my local Wavy Line, handing over a wedge of hard-earned in return for a catering-size bag of barbecue flavoured snacks, a taste for which 'er Indoors has developed ever since she did a night school course in Comfort Eating. I'd just been given the receipt and was about to ask the assistant to make me out a duplicate for 'Goods' (standard business practice which I needn't detain you with here) when some kid with his school cap on backwards and wearing pumps the thickness of an orthopaedic mattress tries to swipe it off me! Turns out he was collecting 'em – not for the Spastics like we did with Co-op Divvy in the old days, and I can tell you they went on some very enjoyable mountaineering holidays courtesy of the Fulham Chapter of the Junior Water Rats – but for a freebie flight into the wide blue yonder for him and his single mother.

My Wotsits chit was the last Godiver's worth he needed, so of course my heart melted, after we'd come to an arrangement regarding a box of Duty Free Monte Cristos. But it set me thinking. This is no way to run an economy and get it revving up in the pits ready for the next millennium! What if *everybody* tried to go on a free Hoover holiday? Nobody would get anywhere! Anarchy!

As my old English teacher used to say, the only place success comes before work is in the dictionary (unless you're reading it backwards, starting with the sports pages). And so here, in the best interests of getting the country back on its plates, is a selection of alumnuses from the Arthur Daley Hall of Fame, pin-ups from my own personal Paella calendar that is kept on permanent display in the lock-up, as an example to us all of what can be achieved through Ingenuity, Industriousness and Integrity – the Three 'I'-d Monster.

ROBERT MAXWELL

The Guvnor. The Nice Big Earner to end them all. War hero, newspaper magnet, saviour of some of our best-loved football clubs, and Spurs . . . it turns my blood to Duckhams 20/50 to read that people not fit to adjust Captain Bob's braces are now hinting that this Colosseum in our midst might not always have played with a straight bat. What did he do that was so heinous, apart from being a Labour MP? Of course, that wasn't exactly the sagest of career moves, seeing as how the Brethren are past masters at sliding their snouts trough-wards. But Bob (or Rudolf Hess as he called himself then) didn't know that, as he'd spent the Conflict on the front line doing his bit by daringly purloining the Third Reich's best dinner services and cutlery and shipping them back to the House of Commons ready for the VE Day celebrations.

But however much he hung out with the big nobs, Bob never forgot his humble origins, refusing to move into a stately pile to which his business ackerman entitled him, and staying put in a council gaff together with his wife and eight kiddies, all kipping together in a chest of drawers. In the best traditions of handing down the family business, Bob also imparted to the sprogs the wisdom he'd picked up along the way, starting with removing a silk handkerchief from a punter's back pocket without attracting attention.

But it was in the golden decade of the 80s that he really came into his own fruition, rescuing the *Daily Mirror* with the famous rallying cry 'Do you seriously want to be rich?' and clearing the pages of knocking copy to make way for the Bingo. Now it's been said in some small-minded quarters that the million pound jackpot on offer was nothing more than print workers' nest eggs salted away for their sunset years. Of course it's very easy to have a go at him now that Mr Maxwell is brown bread, but I would just say two things in his defence. One, did anyone ever actually walk off with a seven-figure gregory? I think not. Second, it was common malpractice for all smudgers in the 80s to do a spot of moonlighting under the monikers Donald Duck and Queen Victoria, so we can do without a lesson on morals from that riff-raff!

Captain Bob however was mortally stung by this hurtful criticism and decided to do the decent thing. After helping rid the world of the red menace by conning old Gorby into setting up an Institute in America that diverted commie gold into the Moonies' pockets instead, Maxwell realised that his life's work on earth was done, and claimed the right of a distinguished military man to bury himself at sea. We that remain can only try and keep his flickering flame alive by following his business methods, speculating to accumulate and making money work for us whenever a Pension Fund should happen to cross our path.

MARK THATCHER

Top-of-the-range businessman, daredevil racing driver, married to a Yank heiress, blessed with the looks of an Adidas, *and* the son of Lady and Lord Thatcher ... why isn't this man our Prime Minister, instead of old Superman in the 'Before' picture? Young Mark is the kind of boy every mother would be proud to see coming up the path for his Sunday lunch, a freshly-signed contract to sell nuclear subs to the Sultan of Brunel tucked into his back pocket. Who can blame his proud Mum for wanting to give the sprog the odd leg-up in life, banging the drum for Britain when we were bidding to provide Johnny Filipino with hot and cold running water? Haven't the knockers ever heard of legal tender? It would surprise me not at all to learn that Maggie picked up her mastery of established business at her father's knee, seeing as he ran a successful corner-shop and would have soon cottoned on that people would pay twopence more for a bag of broken biscuits if they thought they was getting a bargain.

Anyway, Mark has repaid his mother's Large S in buckets and spades by inventing The Thatcher Foundation, something I am investigating myself as a way of whiling away the twilight years and picking up a rich mahogany Desperate Dan at the same time. As far as I can make out (I always get the 'Number Unobtainable' message whenever I try to bell the Foundation) it exists to provide Maggie with a decent gaff in every world capital and beauty spot, somewhere she can relax and get spruced up before mesmerising a Jap Chamber of Commerce or audience of Texas cattle barons, with her memoirs of riding into Goose Green in a Saracen tank after sending General Scargill and his Argies for an early bath.

People the world over are prepared to shell out decent wedges of green- and yellow-backs to hear these tales of derring-do, and Mark is generally on hand to help out with the merchandise of victory: souvenir handbags, Falklands wool, lumps of coal, school milk bottles, etc. As I say, the lecture circuit beckons your truly also, as it occurs to me that beyond these shores a less educated population is thirsting for the inspirational success story. When I mentioned to 'er indoors that I might be away for the odd six winter months bringing comfort to the oppressed, she wanted to come too, as the Denis Thatcher in the scenario. But then I pointed out that the Daley Foundation as yet had no charitable status quo, and she'd be obliged to fork out a whopping single room supplement. That did the trick. As Mark himself might have put it – Mother is the invention of necessity.

DAME SHIRLEY PORTER

'Disgraceful . . . unlawful . . . improper' – these are strong words more befitting to some of my rivals in the quality used motor trade, when a luckless punter discovers that the bargain he's picked up is in fact half of two write-offs from the latest Hogarth Roundabout schemozzle simply welded together (to the warier customer, my advice is to watch out for giveaway brand names on the back of the motor, such as Bentley Allegro, BMW Reliant and so on). Hard to credit, but the above insults were aimed straight at that blameless public servant and philanthropist of this parish, Dame Shirley Porter! And the so-called peccadilly that brought on this torrent of abuse? Rehousing the homeless! And all they were trying to do in return was courteously offer her a vote of thanks!

Of course, one of the less pleasing aspects of the English psycho is that the less successful of us are prone to knock the achievements of others – I myself have been the victim of small-mindedness from the ranks of the desk-bound and visionary-challenged who accuse my tax returns of not being worth the paper they're not written on. How these pygmies must have been waiting to pin something on the heir to the Tesco family fortune, whose motto 'Pile 'em high, sell 'em cheap' were words as meaningful to me as the Lord's Prayer and 'Gentlemen Lift the Seat' when I was a growing lad.

Dame Shirley thought it only fit and proper to follow the same point-of-sale philosophy when it came to disposing of a few unwanted old cemeteries that were cluttering up her manor. As soon as I read the asking price I was round the Westminster Council offices like a bat out of hell as they say in Wisden's Anorak, but I made the crucial error of trying to beat 'em down to 14p per boneyard and thus the chance to extend my empire was put on ice. Nevertheless I think Shirley respected my haggling skills and she said she'd keep in touch if any likely business opportunities came her way in the fullness of time thereof.

Next thing a mysterious anonymous voice comes on the trumpet. 'Arfer,' it says, 'keep this under your titfer, but there's a few one-bedroom gaffs coming vacant any minute round Bayswater way, what d'you reckon? 071 numbers, no rubbish.'

'That's a very tasty carrot,' I says, 'but my and 'er indoors's roots are in Fulham now and we're a bit long in the tooth to start learning new closing times at the local offies.'

'No one's asking you to live there – just get your name on the electoral register. We're looking for Upwardly Mobile couples who know which side their bread's buttered on come election day if you get my drift. That describes you and 'er, doesn't it?'

'Yes, but . . .'

'Good, I'll put you down for three,' says the voice. 'Let me know if you want a motor to the polling station.'

As it happens I did pop round one afternoon to see the gaffs and very tasty they looked too, from the outside. (I couldn't see in because all the doors and windows had been steel-shuttered courtesy of that retired plod John Stalky who wants you to trust him.) Now suddenly the brown stuff's hit the fan and Dame Shirley and her cahoots are accused of being in cohorts with someone called Gerry Mander. I could have told her – start dealing with Irishmen and you're in for nothing but grief.

LESTER PIGGOTT

When the history of this great nation comes to be written (and speaking as someone whose name is down to be at the very least a large footnote in the Business Section, if not an actual pull-out) I am ashamed to say there will be a couple of very big blots on the pages dealing with our renowned sense of Fair Play and Justice. You've got an Halleluyah Chorus of voices crying out from people who've been wrongly banged up in jug, whether it's your Birmingham 6, nicked for speaking with horrible accents, or the Long Fellow himself, the Housewives' Choice and doyen of Derby Day, Lester Piggott OBE.

You'll note that I'm calling him by his full and correct nomenclature: after all it was to Her Majesty

*The Author having a quiet word
in the more operational of
Lester's shell-likes.*

herself to whom Lester bent the knee to receive his gong (in fact in view of the height involved she bent down to him), richly deserved for Services to the Small Punter. But then, in a total transvestite of justice, said honour was rudely ripped from his chest, re-struck and pinned to somebody else, most likely a snake-hipped pop singer on Di's Walkman. All I can say is, the Royals were being very badly advised, probably by the same geezer who told Prince Philip that it'd be a hoot to call the Chinks slitty-eyed. The Japs, that's a different matter.

Because, let's face it, what was Lester's deadly sin? He showed the Inland Revenue a clean pair of heels, leaving them panting in his wake as he shot round Tottenham Corner, laughing all the way to the Swiss bank. Not that he didn't put his hands up when the men in the Mr Byrite suits turned up on his doorstep one day with the milk – he offered to cough up the thirty-five years' arrears there and then. Sad to say the silly boy chose to pay 'em out of his Under The Floorboards account, as endorsed by the likes of Ken Dodd. Doddy got off with it by charming the beak with his tickling stick and leaving the revenue men performing a heartfelt rendering of 'Tears for souvenirs are all you've left me' but Lester wasn't so lucky. When asked 'Is that all your declared income, or what?' he replied 'What?' on account of being mutt-and-jeff.

This however led to Lester's master-stroke. When detained at HMP, instead of climbing on the roof and frisbeeing slates like the other bird-doers, he planned to make use of the freeing up of the Telecom lines and create a tipping service. Result, a classic earner which maximised the Piggott speciality – incomprehensible-ness – as you discovered when you belled his 0891 number and after half an hour at peak rate, the race was long gone and you *still* couldn't work out which pony he fancied!

THE ENTERPRISE CULTURE
The Green, Green Shoots of Home

'The world's workshop' is just one of the many epaulets attached to the UK. Ever since Napoleon, or Boney N, got in a sulk after being beaten by Sandie Shaw in the Eurovision Song Contest and left us to invent the cross-Channel ferry, we have been a byword in enterprise. You'd got Joe Wedgewood turning out his pyrex dishes, while over in India Ramsay Macdonald was educating the natives in the possibilities of their sacred animal, the cow. They'd never thought of it served up with a pickle and mustard. Talk about Open Sesame Seed Bun!

These days though we'd be hard pushed to sell a can of lager in an Australian desert. There was a time in the entrepreneurial Eighties when we were on the straight and narrow, as under the watchful gaze of Lady T the means of production was returned to those with the know-how to run a business and a wedge to stump up for the shares. We didn't put as much lucre up the Exchequer's way and we were shelling out on VCRs, CDs and all manner of goods as fast as we in the import/export trade could supply them.

So what happened? Well, the first nail in the camel's coffin was the ditching of Maggie. As she and Denis, her Eminence Grease, drove out of Downing Street, all our get-up-and-go – the Falklands Spirit that our brave boys in their shell-suits did so much to fight for – got up and went with 'em. And what have we got now? A trapeze artist from across the water. Euro-bastards as far as the eye can see. For VCRs read ecus. And as for the geezers still having a go, dipping their thumbs in the worldwide business pie trying to pull out a plum for Blighty – we only stick the likes of Ernest Saunders and Gerald Ronson in nick and force them to make their own phone-cards. There was a time we'd have put up a statue.

As the old saying goes: if a fish stinks it ain't from the tail up. And that's the problem. Nobody wants to plant the seedlings from which the tender shoots of recovery will grow. No one is prepared to exchange the belt of expectation today for the braces of the pay-off tomorrow. Even if they do they've got to contend with the lurking menace laying in wait on the other side of the so-called Channel Tunnel, with their crèches, statutory lunch hours and social contracts (or rabies, to put it another way). How is Britain meant to get back on its feet if it can't exploit anybody or anything?

'Hold up, Arthur,' I hear you say. 'If you can't

ARTHUR DALEY PLC
EURODALEY
ARTHUR DALEY LANDSCAPE GARDENING LTD
HE WELSH DEVELOPMENT OFFICE
ULHAM BRANCH)
THE DALEY ESCORT AGENCY
THE DALEY CORTINA AGENCY
AAAAAAARTHUR FIRST-IN-THE-YELLOW-PAGES
R REPAIRS
EY KWALITY
ICATIONS NETWORK
NDERSON DALEY
NT CONSULTANTS
INGS LTD
OOKING-AFTER-FOR-A-PAL LTD
N-BRAND DRY GOODS
X HEALTH AUTHORITY (FULHAM BRANCH)
INE COACHES FOR SAREJEVO

My pride and joy. The family jewels. Each and every one the Golden Delicious of my eye. There isn't a seat on the board of any of 'em which wouldn't grace an ex-Junior Minister's pin-striped bottom! (At the time of writing there are in fact one or two good seats still available, a monkey each and no questions asked as they say in Parliament.)

tip us the wink to the future well-being of this semi-precious stone set on a silver platter, then who can?' And you would be bang on the money to ask, seeing as how 'being one step ahead of the competition' is my recreation in *Who's Who* (I send in my entry every year, regular as clockwork – I reckon it's bound to come up sooner or later, like Ernie bonds). So here is my personal blue book of pointers to prosperity.

SOUTH BY SOUTH-WEST

Everyone's been having a go at real estate, but pay no heed. It's not what you put up, but where you put it. The gaff can have won every prize going, but if the post code is suspect then you're going to be stuck with a well-weatherbeaten To Let sign. You can have the plushest offices in London – glass lifts, commission-aires with both arms, toilet doors going all the way down to the floor – but put them on the Isle of Dogs and you might as well be on Devil's Island or Sark, because it's going to be just as hard getting up West for that four-course expenses-paid lunch over which all important business is transacted. Can you imagine Richard Branson or Sir Alan Hansen carving up the money markets over a dog roll and a cuppa, shoulder to shoulder with some loudmouth sherbert helmsman? I think not.

Location is the key, and the key to location is water, so watch out for Fulham Wharf. It's got the lot. Lick of paint and some plasterboard and you could have a flat fit for a coffee ad. It's got a natural deep-water harbour for your top international business-man's yacht, or you could land your helicopter down Hurlingham. There's plenty of potential office space with short lets no problem. All it needs is a smart little eaterie run by some rude nutter in a white hat and a regular celebrity clientele like Michael Caine or Sue Pollard and the carriage trade would pour in.

Now all of you in bandit country up the M6, those that can read, might think this was too easy. My advice is: you get yourselves down to the Smoke and take a butcher's for yourselves. Give the punters a comfy pew, a view of the water and a two-foot-long menu and you can charge a tenner for chips with fish an optional extra. This goes for anybody with access to a pond or reservoir – get yourself some planning permission. The more unspoilt it is the better. It's a deep-seated desire beating in every true Englishman's chest to look out at a bit of natural beauty, especially if you've got car parking.

CAN PAY, DON'T PAY

Budding adventure capitalists could do a lot worse than follow the example set by Lord Archer of Victoria. Finding himself boracic one night and in urgent need of £2000 in readies, what did he do? Sat down and wrote a best-seller about being boracic and in urgent need of readies! Jeffrey never looked back and now has a flat overlooking the river, a country house once occupied by Rupert Bear, a lovely wife who bangs the dinner-gong at Lloyd's and a perfect complexion. Turning your own experiences into an earner is deeply satisfying and can only be compared to selling a punter the same resprayed motor you bought off him six weeks earlier.

I have decided therefore to offer my own expertise in a particularly thistly field, viz. brown envelopes from the Inland Revenue arriving every morning with the milk. Because without doubt one of the greatest burdens to rebuilding the economy is the punitive tax system. You see, money these days is all-electric – jumping from one currency to another on them little computers you see on the telly news, while ex-barrow boys shout the odds and throw paper darts at each other. Cash went out with Johnny Haynes and long shorts. I tried to explain this the other day when I had a visit from one of Whitehall's sternest who was quizzing me over my finances and pointing out that 'tax returns' didn't mean I should just send them back unopened. Naturally I gave as good as I got, and here's a transcript of our free and frank discussion, an appetiser for my forthcoming manual which will really make the likes of John Harvey-Smith sit up and take notice, or at least get a decent haircut.

'Mr Daley,' (he says), 'you seem to pay no income tax at all and yet you have a company and company assets. For example a Jaguar car.'

'That's not mine. You've got that all wrong. That's my uncle's. I said to him, Sid, why do you need a car like that, I said. I mean, you being an old age pensioner, I said. I just keep it for him. It's an old man's folly. And do you know what he said? You use it Arthur, he said. You not having wheels of your own. Wasn't that nice, eh?'

'But you do use the car for work?'

'Work? A man of my age? They don't want mature, experienced men like me. No, I use the motor to take old folk down the Darby and Joan Club. People who have to go to the hospital. Or at election time. No favours. If they want to vote – even if it's for some loony lefty – I'll take them down to the polling station. I'm into good deeds, charity. Incidentally – have you got the time?'

'Quarter past twelve.'

'Thank you. What a lovely kettle, I mean watch.

I wish I could have a simple watch. But these days
. . . well, it's just an extravagance these days.'

'Maybe you'll find one in your lock-up.'

'My lock-up? Is this the reason for the interrogation?
I have hobbies.'

'Hobbies?'

'I make things. Toys mainly. Toys for deprived
children.'

'One of my staff called at your lock-up and said
it was full of boxes.'

'Ah, now, I can mark your card about them. They
were some curios. Flood-damaged swimming cos-
tumes and speaking dollies, made in Taiwan and
speaking Taiwanese. I tinker with them, repair them
for a pittance, that sort of thing.'

'A pittance?'

'Nothing to pay income tax on.'

'Could I ask you how you get by, what with rent,
food, clothes, the occasional drink?'

'I often ask myself that. Bingo I suppose.'

'*Bingo? !*'

'All down to 'er indoors. She manages well.'

'Little Metro, two children at a private
school . . .'

'I don't know how she does it. Just between
you and me, I think she's got a few pennies in
the Post Office.'

'I suppose she has, Mr Daley . . .'

A broken man, he gave me some spare change for
a cup of tea, made an excuse and left.

CAPTAINS OUTRAGEOUS

There's been a lot of unseemly brouhaha of late about the size of the wage packets being taken home to the missus every Friday by the captains of our great denationalised industries – gas, water, the dog. Sour grapes, say I. It's crystal to me that anyone who can devote his life to making Margate beach fit for kiddies to play on by clearing it of unmentionable elements (and I don't mean Germans) is worth every penny spent. And as for British Telecom, that's been completely transmogrified. Take phone boxes – they've gone from being the old red eyesores, full of jimmy riddle and chip papers, to state-of-the-art open-plan business centres, bursting with exciting invitations and opportunities. And that's just the postcards stuck in the fittings! What's more, the competition with Mercury has opened up a whole new era of merchandising.

Suddenly, now they're not legal tender no more, the Chelsea Antiques Fair mob can't get enough of bakelite phones, demob suits, Arthur English moustaches – it'll be gas masks next, you mark my words. One way and another, it's all a very salivatory lesson in exploiting the country's natural resources: withdraw the supply, create the demand then market the

Eartha Kitt out of it. I've got a couple of score red phone boxes in the lock-up, any takers?

EUROPE
Gateway to Folkestone

Amid all the Euroargy-bargy and Bruges breugas
of late, one burning question seems to have gone
between the goalie's legs and slipped through the
net unanswered: what have we got in common with
Them Over There in the first place? Do the Germans
play rugby, do the French play cricket, do the Dutch
play football? Nein. Non. Nog. As far as the Man on
the Privatised Clapham Omnibus is concerned, our
heritage and emotional tie is with the Commonwealth
countries to whom we have given the greatest gifts of
all to: democracy and decent plumbing. Nations who
have earned the right to vote after years of carefully
controlled economic activity with the motherland,
and who have vouchsafed us in return everything
that the great rubik 'Made in Hong Kong' stands for.
Who else in Europe can say they had an empire? The
Belgian Congo is like copping the Old Kent Road on
the monopoly board. Who had your Park Lanes, your
Mayfairs and your Marylebone Stations? Blighty,
right.

Now what this means of course is that we are
a mature and sensible country well sorted to offer

the European continent – who let's face it is still adjusting its dress after being ravaged by the Hun, and before that Hannibal – all the accumulated nous at our disposal. But does it pay us any attention or respect? Again, *nul points*! In fact quite the opposite. At every turn of the autobahn Europe is plotting our downfall. Only the other day Jack De Lorean tried to kibosh one of the great traditions that must have had Charlie Dickens triple salko-ing in his grave: child labour, or to give it its much more dignified English moniker, Young Adult Entrepreneurship. The man is only trying to stamp out the freedom of the press by stopping boys and girls delivering your daily linens! Doesn't he understand that the Industrial Revolution was built upon such childish endeavours? Teenage chimney-sweeps who became captains of industry like Sir Terence Habitat, tiny tots down the mines who blossomed into England fast bowlers – and of course my own career batting for Britain's industry began in those formative years, following the milkman's horse round with a bucket and spade. What greater testimonial can I offer than that?

The time has never been riper for the enlightened businessman to exploit opportunities for a decent return on his sub. The giant beer-moth of the trade union movement had its wings well and truly clipped by the sword of St Maggie, and there are plenty of willing workers ready to pedal the length of the land to cop £1.50 an hour, anything legal considered. But what does De Lorean and his crew, all steel bins and Samsonite briefcases, do? They whack out some directive from hell called the Social Charter, divided up into chapters headed 'Training Your Labour', 'Overtime Begins at 40' and 'Hot Air Hand Dryers in the Loos'. What good would training do – to take a random example – my lad? He needs on-the-job experience. And in our line of high-pressure graft at the coal-face you can't work statutory hours – you have to seize the main chance, often under cover of darkness.

The other great Beecher's Brook for handsome trade across the Channel is the language. Just what effort are our so-called Euro-cousins making to learn the Queen's English? Now I know in Amsterdam they reckon to speak it better than Dave, not to mention understanding it, but our next-door neighbours the French take a very dim view of the Mother Tongue and are trying to excommunicate such anglicisations as 'Le Weekend' and 'Le quarter-pounder'. I ask you: what hope can there be for a business agreement if the participants at the meet don't allow international *bon mots justes* known and respected the world over like 'Le back-handeur' and 'Le brown envelope de readies'?

Another import we certainly want to rebuff, dearie me yes, is European culture. They have morals looser

Me pictured shortly after handing over a petition full of signatures (many of them different) protesting about the Social Chapter. This plain-clothes plod who accepted it on behalf of the PM was most civil and even invited me in for 'a cup of tea, or not tea'. Diet Lilt, it turned out to be.

than post-ruby bowels over there, and have already tried to corrupt our young with daily doses of Eyetie housewife pulchritude via spy satellites. Picture 'er indoors doing a striptease and entwining herself round the standard lamp in the lounge, and you get a good idea of this menace from the skies. It was an uplifting experience to see that our Government and the gentlemen of the popular press rose as one man against this tidal wave of degradation. Thank God for Richard Murdoch! Single-handedly he's seen to it that instead of sleaze, the satellite channels are stuffed to the gunnels with wholesome quality entertainment like *The Partridge Family* and *The Flying Nun*. He's also introduced the decoder system, so the kiddies can't accidentally be exposed to X-rated entertainment like the England cricket tour.

We need more of this constant vigilance – imagine the impact on our watering holes of Cafe Society! I shiver as I contemplate the prospect of patrons of the Winchester lounging under Martini umbrellas sipping pina colladas and buying single roses for the trouble from gyppos with baskets. With our narrow pavements there'd be nowhere for me to park the Jag of course, but this is a fundamental bone of contention that goes right to the heart of our essential Britishness: the tradition of the public house complete with the cosy bonhomie of an all-male environment, microwaved Cornish pasties, sausages too long for the plate and not an ice cube in sight speaks for this country with all the eloquence and melody of a Shakespeare ballad.

In a nutshell then, our wits are going to have to be well kept about us if we aren't to become just another pasteurised region in the United States of Europe. If the Twelve, or the Sixteen or however many it is (see, they haven't even been taught to add up properly) want to play ball, they have to learn that it's *our* ball they'll be playing with, and we have the right of veto and taking it home.

I'm happy to say that moves are already afoot to show Friend Euro who's in the driving seat with regard to the train now departing from Gay Paree to London Waterloo. Except we've moved the goal-posts, up to St Pancras. These delaying tactics show the kind of expertise for which we're justly famous: confusing the enemy and then stealing their shoes while they're a-kip. If the French had their way there'd be some orange monstrosity hurtling through the Home Counties at the speed of light, upsetting the cows and putting old war heroes and retired comedians off their golf swings. But it is not to be.

When passengers on the Chunnel Express, all Burberries and Brut aftershave, hit our shores they will have to abide by our local customs, and transfer to Grade 1 listed rolling stock, so called because of the movement of beer cans up and down the aisles. A gentle trundle through the Garden of England, paying due care and attention to flora and fauna on the line and the traditional signals failure at Ashford, and they're in sight of the 'Welcome to Britain' Union Jack tea-towels waved by cheerful Cockneys out of their back doors. But not quite. Thanks to the Government's far-sighted No Through Ticketing policy they'll all have to disembark at East Croydon for a passport control check, delousing and body search, and then pay an additional fare into London, purchased from a designated kiosk marked Le Arm et Le Leg. Queueing for same will give your average foreign businessman some much-needed humility and a starter pack in the English way of doing things. So don't reset your watch Monsieur, as you emerge blinking into the crisp Kent air wafting across from Dungeness: over here you'll always be an hour behind!

INTERNATIONAL POLITICS
Dog Day Weekend

You will not be surprised to hear that I pride myself on being something of a Tonto when it comes to the world political situation, keeping my ear to the ground at all times and a beady eye on smoke signals which tell the more hirsute among us which way the wind's blowing. This Salmon Rushton business to give you a for-instance. House arrest may be just what the doctor ordered for the likes of 'er indoors, but it is quite beyond the pail in a civilised society that a best-selling author has to black up and don beard and bins every time he wants to exercise his citizen's right to appear on late-night telly. I too know what it's like to be under siege, and I intend to relate my experiences here in the hope that it may bring comfort to hostages everywhere, whether in the Saudi of Arabia or banged up by the Brum plod.

It all started the day I'd been to see my dentist, Pete the Pliers as he's known in the trade, to have the regular MOT on my hampsteads. A winning smile is *de rigger*, one of the first reassurances a punter needs when stepping gingerly onto the forecourt, and it is of no commercial value whatsoever if said smile is disfigured by a couple of black and cavernous gaps. Whether it was Pete's gas being turned up too high, or an industrial-strength VAT that Dave mixed for me (there's a first time for everything) when I repaired to the Winchester to soothe my tender gums, or a lethal cocktail of both, I found myself coming over all woozy and agreeing to an extremely dubious proposition. Even my old boxing pal No-Nose Norrington would have smelt a rat.

'Geezer over there wants to stash five grand away for the weekend, Arthur,' said Dave, pointing out a cove whose boat lacked only a pencil moustache for him to have the word 'Spiv' stamped in his passport. 'The way I see it, you could cop for a handy wedge of commission and reduce your bar bill, which at this moment in time is rubbing shoulders with the Mexican National Debt.'

'Setting aside for the minute any trifling sums I may inadvertently have chalked up on the slate, Dave,' I replied haughtily, 'What's wrong with sticking it in the peter in your back room?'

'Do what?' Dave exploded with a guffaw, indicating the Winchester clientele with a sweep of his arm, and I was forced to agree he had a point – the cast of an entire edition of *Crimewatch* was arrayed before us, not one of them without the ink of a fingerprint pad under their nails, and that was just the women.

The up and down of it was, Dave introduced me

to this bloke, one Tony Loretto, and I found myself agreeing to billet his cash in my lock-up till Monday morning in return for a monkey, no questions asked. This you may think was my first mistake, but as far as I'm concerned trust is like planting tomatoes: it either bears fruit or withers on the vine, in which case you resort to Gro-bags. Where I did put a foot in something iffy was in indemnifying him against loss, or to put it in plain English, if the dibs did a runner it was my neck.

I'm surprised Dave let me drive home after that, but set off into the night I did. The Jag must have been purring a lullaby into my ears like the 'Skye Boat Song' that the Jocks sing when they've done us at Twickers, because suddenly – wallop! I hit something. Picture the emotions raging like a torrent through my fuddled senses. No-claims bonus up the Swanee. The Daley name dragged through the courts. Character witnesses suddenly all on holiday. The patriotic Union Jack, fluttering proudly above Daley Motors, hauled down by an ugly mob and replaced by the skull-and-crossbones. And what – oh my Gawd – if they were brown bread? For a moment of eternity I sat there like Michael Aspro and his Big Red Book, someone else's life flashing before me.

I was more relieved than Mafeking to discover when I got out that what I had struck a glancing blow was a big dog, which lay there looking up at me sad and resentful with huge wet minces – not a million miles from the reception I occasionally get from 'er indoors after a good night at the Winchester, when I'm hopping about the bedroom with both legs down one jim-jam. Then it gets to its feet and starts whimpering for its owner – and we both see this geezer looking over his shoulder as he scarpers down the road.

Before I can stop it the dog's jumped up into my front passenger seat and looks like it's settled in for the night. Then one more strange thing occurs. A van that's seen better days – in fact even if it was a Roman chariot in a previous existence it must have been a write-off – comes hurtling round the corner on two wheels. Packed into the front are three blokes with faces set like Mount Rushmore, and off they go in the direction of the first geezer. Me, I head back for the Winchester.

'You're not leaving that thing here,' says Dave, wearing his Good Samaritan hat as usual. 'It looks to me like one of those Japanese fighting dogs – towsers or whatever they call 'em.' As it happened the dog *was* looking a bit slitty-eyed as it sat up on a bar stool, its paws round the Guinness tap.

'That's because it's tired,' I said. 'Dog-tired,' quipped my boy, who'd just come in with a big bag of mixed biscuits he'd picked up from one of my network of wholesalers. And sure enough it lays down its head on the bar, as to the manner born of many a Winchester customer, and drifts into a deep kip.

'That's it – out!' orders Dave. 'Arthur – you've got to take it home.'

'Dave – you might as well give me a hydrochloric acid-and-tonic,' I said. 'Because that's what my life'll be worth if I as much as walk up the path in company with man's best friend. 'Er indoors is allergic to anything with more than two legs. It all dates back to her childhood when she was frightened by a milkman's horse who tried to eat the flower in her hat and nearly took a piece of her ear with it. Her old man was going to take the company to court but they settled for a year's free milk. Then he bought her another hat and told her to hang round the front gate again . . .'

This fascinating social history was rudely interrupted by a commotion at the end of the bar. One of the clientele had mistaken the bowl my boy had filled with dog biscuits for bar snacks, and had been tucking in. One or two of the others got the taste for them and now they were squabbling over the last one. Not to mention calling for more sherbets because the biscuits had given 'em a right Geoff Hurst. Dave looked at me and I could see those pound signs in his eyes as we both sensed a serendipitious earner. The upshot was the dog had a temporary home.

'Tell you what, Arthur,' pipes up my boy, 'if it is a fighting dog it needs to be registered. Why not have a look inside its ear to see if it's got an identity tag?'

'As the man said at the Hackney bus stop, this is what we call a Catch-22 situation,' I said. 'If I go rummaging around in its shell-like and it turns out there *is* a tag in there, then I'll be in a unique position to take on the role of Captain Hook in the next Fulham Arts Theatre production of *Peter Pan*. I think we should let sleeping dogs lie.'

But mention of the aforesaid Boy Who Never Grew Up, that turn-of-the century Gazza, gave me a brainwave and next day I was off to see Pete the Pliers again, who got the dog into his dentist's chair and X-rayed its ear. Nothing there except fur. But on the way out we were stopped by a punter who put down the middle eight pages of a 1973 copy of *Titbits* he'd been reading and forgot all about his throbbing gob in his excitement. 'That's a very fine example of a Staffordshire bull terrier you've got there, squire,' he says. 'Worth a few bob, I can tell you.'

'You mean – pedigree, chum?' I ask, which happy fact he confirms. So now it's back to the lock-up to guard my asset, stopping off at the Winchester to discover from my boy that my wholesaler has agreed to a flat rate of £500 for the entire consignment of dog biscuits, to be known henceforth as Daley's Old

Granary Snacks. You're no doubt one step ahead of me now: this monkey was the very sum Loretto was bunging me for the use of my gaff. The weekend was proceeding sweet as a nut!

Remembering the villains in the van, I deemed it only right and proper that we should set about ascertaining the dog's rightful owners, as there would no doubt be a reward in the offing. Dave got his Polaroid out from behind the bar, the one he's wont to use later on during one of the Winchester's 'themed evenings', Salute to Judy Garland and the like – the resulting compromising pictures he reckons will one day be as good as a pension. A few tastefully posed studies of the dog on a stool and my boy was off round all the breeders in a ten-mile radius, while I go back to the lock-up to start planning the cornering of the snacks market – on your penny-farthing, Phineas Fogg!

Next thing Dave's on the trumpet in a right tiz. He'd had a visit from the heavy mob in the van, who apparently made loan sharks look like coy carp. They were after their dog and were threatening to relandscape the Winchester, starting with Dave's face. The gaff had been blown by the ashtray in the Polaroids with the Winchester's name on it, which we'd thoughtfully filled with water and given to the dog to lap up, seeing as how he wouldn't touch the biscuits. Dave's a great believer in the old Muslim

saying 'Discretion's the better part of Allah' and so
he'd told 'em where they could lay their hands on
their property, not to mention yours truly. The man's
a saint.

So the lock-up was about to be in a Rorke's
Drift situation. There was no way I could get in
touch with my boy for protection – his car-phone
had been cut off after a bit of grief about paying the
jack-and-jill (I'd get him to reverse the charges and
claimed that if he was within the Greater London
area, which he always was, it should count as a 10p
local call, what's so heinous about that?). The dog
and I were on first-name or at any rate face-licking
terms by this time and he wouldn't budge when I
tried to release him into Fulham's wide open spaces.
So I barricaded myself in. Luckily the dog biscuits
were there to keep me going, and I thawed out a
couple of dozen frozen spam fritters I'd had ready
for the celebration of the D-Day landings, to keep
'im indoors's tail wagging.

First the witching hour passed, then the hour
the Winchester closes, then the hour it *really* closes.
Nothing. But then the old cherry-hog started to growl.
Someone was trying to get in the lock-up via the
tradesman's entrance, through the tiny skylight at
the back. It can't have been any of those geezers I saw
in the van, I thought, not unless they've spent the last
six hours in a clinic up St John's Wood having all the

fat sucked out of them. So I click on the light, the dog pounces and there cowering in my Home Entertainments Centre, between the boxes of CD players and the clock-radios, is a kid in a balaclava with a skier on it.

He tries to stay stumm but the dog bares its teeth, with bits of pink spam fritter stuck between 'em, which I told him was all that was left of the last kid who tried to turn my place over. That does the trick and he confesses he's the son of Loretto, the geezer whose five grand I'm guarding. Suddenly both pieces fall into place like an Irish jigsaw. I do a Ken Dodd and lift the floorboard whereunder the money is hid, screw in an eyepiece like my namesake Arthur Nougat off the Antiques Roadshow and *voila!* Five thousand pieces of forged paper!

It seems these Lorettos have seen *Maverick* and decided to be modern day con-artists on paddleboats on the Mississippi, except this is Old Father Thames. They find some mug punter eager to make a quick commish (present whistle-blowing company excepted, naturally) then stitch him up. I'm just taking notes from the kid on the precise machinery of these scams – so I can warn the less intellectually blessed – when a familiar van barges its way into the lock-up without bothering to knock. Out jump the Brothers Grim and demand the return of their whimpering pooch who is now cowering behind his adopted Dad.

'You shall not pass,' I say. 'Dog-fighting is a wicked travesty of a sport second only to running non-triers at Windsor races.'

'Who said anything about fighting?' said the one who looked most able to get his words out without dribbling. 'We want to breed Arnold there.'

'What with?' I asked dubiously, knowing that these men of Essex extraction get up to some pretty strange practices out in the Gants Hill hinterland.

'A bitch of course,' he said. 'There's a prize Staffordshire that's in town for one weekend only and she's on heat. See – we've got the pedigree certificate.' And he waves this official-looking document in front of me.

Suddenly the Loretto kid reaches out, grabs it and before we can do anything he's out of the lock-up like sugar off a shovel. A lightbulb big enough to illuminate Regent Street at Christmas came on above my head.

'Take a seat, gents,' I said, 'and tell me what the geezer who owned this bitch looked like.'

So that was the Great Siege of the Lock-Up, which all ended happily, barring a severe outbreak of the trots which sore afflicted all those unwise enough to have partaken of Daley's Old Granary Snacks, the proprietor included. Perhaps it doesn't compare with the five years that Paul McCartney was incarcerated by the towel-heads, but I've no doubt that 'er indoors would have risen to the occasion and organised a Friends of Arthur Daley Campaign, complete with badges and vigils and heartfelt appeals from assorted bags of yeast. I am of course available to go on the chat-show circuit at the drop of a trilby, though 'er might need a personal call from that Irishman in the irish himself before she's tempted out.

THE DECLINE OF THE SOVIET BLOC AND ITS GEOPOLITICAL AND ECONOMIC IMPLICATIONS

As I stand here, if you did a Harris Poll round the Winchester (which would not be a long job on account of there only being two geezers called Harris) there would be no arguments about the single most important event of the last ten years. Not the decision to play Rugby League at Craven Cottage, but the dramatic collapse of the Communist world. Well of course it would be, I hear you say: its impact was monumental and epic.

And you would be right: it means no more of those dodgy East European motors in orange and turquoise eating away at our much-cherished used car market!

Needless to say I was in pole position when the Berlin Wall did a Jericho, ready to liberate Ivan and Boris from the nightmare world of travelling ten to a Trabant and having to join a waiting list to get their names on a windshield. I have made it my personal crusade, vowing not to rest until every ex-commie has access to his own Airbag!

EDUCATION
A Class Act

When you get to my august age in life it allows you the luxury of surveying the vesta of your past from a high green hill. And across the valleys and lakes of experience there stands out an unspoilt dingly dell of violet flowers with little deer and rabbits and field mice in waistcoats running around in it: the old school days.

Like many of our nation's national figures I too have been through the white-water rapids of an institutional education. Although, straight up I have to say mine didn't require wearing the old titfer or singing the Eton Boating Song. The Hammersmith Blowing Up Frogs Down By The Reservoir Song would be nearer the mark. But like all of the Blade-on-the-Feather brigade, I too was instilled with the sense of pride in our green and pleasant land and the ingrained commitment to public duty that characterfies the life of so many great patriots.

But what of today's youth? When they bunk off school are they generating a few bob for the balance of trade ledger or sowing the seeds of future prosperity? No, it's straight round some flea-infested arcade to play with their sonic hamster!

And when they leave the old alma cogan, do they learn a trade? Not likely – it's either signing up for the Old-King-Cole or off to Hertfordshire to play on a computer for some multinational insurance company. In my day your average school leaver went and did something socially useful, like becoming a mechanic, keeping the nation on the road, and if they were very handy they could carry out the heart surgery of the motor trade. Now there are those men of little vision under their peaked caps who think slapping together two halves of different cars is a bit rum. But it's just recycling, to use a buzz word much enamoured of the nattering classes. And apart from the environmental benefits there's the wealth creation angle to consider: workers needed, readies flowing through the arteries of the economy and a few bob in it for whoever is this week's Chancellor of the Exchequer.

But no one becomes an artisan these days unless they've got GCHQs. When I was a nipper, unless you had bins and a slide rule you failed your exams and you went off to work. Only the cream de la crop got to wear tweed jackets and scarves and shout yoiks at the Boat Race. The rest of us was earning a crust. Everyone knew their place, everything was in order. Now, every spotty teenager has got a third degree, and where's it got us?

Look at crime. Society gets the villains it deserves. Mark my words. In the old days smart lads joined up with firms and did a little thieving. Did his apprenticeship as watchout, learnt his craft. Bit of initiative and he could nick the getaway car, maybe even drive it (or so I'm told). A cruise down The Listening Bank, make 'em pay attention by waving a sawn-off around and hop it with a bag of notes, in and out like a fiddler's elbow. Or if it was a jeweller's, into The Fiddler's Elbow itself, famous for having more fences than the Three Musketeers. End result? No harm done to the peaceable citizenry like me and you, unless you happened to be The Man from the Pru.

But now, because they've all got exams, young lads turn their noses up at the old family business. So there's your infrastructure up the spout and the gang bosses are forced to import cheap foreign labour with shooters and Stanley knives down their socks. A lot of nastiness, in other words. And what's the root cause? Too much modern progressive education!

That's why I'm a keen advocate of involving the private sector in our future thinking, to wit appointing prominent local businessmen to the boards of school governors. I for one am looking forward to offering the budding youth of Fulham a guiding light down the rocky and often perilous road of their lives. And with the financial blight that seems to have hit the schools, who better than a successful entrepreneur to help the headmistress sort the books and make that council grant go a bit further, instead of lying idle in a bank account over the weekend?

Talking of tomes for learning I can also supply barely used geography textbooks at competitive pre-decimalisation prices. What's more all the countries will be coloured in pink and have their proper names, none of your Botswanias or Mugabes. And with my many contacts in the local community I can be of enormous help when it comes to giving the old building a lick of paint, so long as it's institutional green (as I sit here in the lock-up writing this), or fixing them up with some one-owner-only roofing slate. When you reach my age you realise the importance of giving as well as taking. I tell you, I'm a knight on a white charger for our chalky mortar-boarded brethren.

And what do I ask in return for this lycanthropy? Merely the use of a few of the likeliest lads in the school, to come and study at Daley Motors on day release. Here they'll be trained in fieldwork of the highest calibre which will set them up for a career that's right there among life's highest callings. Like the Jesus-ites say: 'Give me a boy at seven and he's my boy for the duration'.

Even the National Curriculum McVities is right up my street. It's all very well asking what the square root of C is if it's divided by X times a pie. But what use is that in the real world? Here's more the sort of thing:

Practical Mathematics, Stage 1

1) If Simple Simon has a thousand battery-operated football rattles at a Lady Godiver apiece wholesale, and you're in for a gross of that . . . what's the value of his remaining stock?

© Daley Academy of Hard Knocks
– Pub Quiz Nights Also Catered For

You see, that's the sort of maths any bright spark is going to have to juggle with on the market stall of life. And if you want to be management, a decision maker, then these problems have to be your meat and drink. Otherwise you wind up like my boy, whose prospects are but a short pier in the long walk of his existence, with hardly the money to buy water wings.

Here endeth the lesson.

HEALTH
Mens Sana in Corporate Hospitality

As my dear old mother used to say: you haven't got nothing if you haven't got your health. Although of course Howard Hughes (my spiritual father) might disagree as he seemed to have everything but. I dare say that was on account of his penchant for hot dogs, Jane Russell's cleavage, and oxygen tents. Very dodgy. Then again, look at Tsar Nicholas's little lad. Set fair to inherit the Mother of all Russias but a haemophiliac. He only had to graze his knee falling off his scooter and he was off to Casualty with a couple of bags of juice hooked up over the royal bed. Mind you, as we well know, things didn't work out too clever on the inheritance front anyway. No, there can be no question that good health is a fundamental part of living a long and prosperous life.

These days we take it all for granted. GPs on call, ambulances with all mod cons and their names spelt backwards, fresh-faced nurses with bedpan eyes, young doctors with bags under theirs. But it wasn't always like this. In medieval times if you got an itch they stuck a leech on you, and made you drink all sorts of concoctions not even Dave has ever mixed

to sort out your gout. And if your appendix started playing up – well, you could forget about a quick ride down to the operating table and loophole surgery. You'd be pushing up the daisies and not so much as a whiff of a life insurance policy to tide over the missus until your sons and heirs were old enough to go into servitude.

Life in those days was like sticking all your hard earned on a rank outsider to win at 20–1. You either came up trumps or you were nowhere. There was no NHS to offer up a nice little each-eay bet, take out your tonsils or whip in a triple bypass. One minute you're tilling the land, the next you're under it. And it wasn't much better by the eighteenth century, what with those dodgy jocks Burke and Hare (aka the Edinburgh Two) digging up the dearly departed so that Doctor Finlay's great grandfather could cut them open and see how it all worked. But could he put them back together again? By the time he'd finished, half the dead bodies looked like the engine compartment of a Skoda Estelle after my lad's been tinkering with it. No wonder they called the place Old Reekie. But medical science needs to investigate to progress: even today young medical students examine corpses. They should get themselves down to Fulham for a home game, it'd be a lot easier.

But if there wasn't progress what a sorry state we'd be in. If you broke your leg in days of yore you didn't wake up to find Doctor Johnson writing best wishes on your plaster of Paris with his quill – it was hacked off. Imagine that now. You're having a game of park footy, a bit of a rough tackle comes in, snap! Down the local apothecary's they give you a double gin without the tonic, whip out the Black and Decker and next thing you know you're going to fancy dress parties as Douglas Bader. There would be a national outcry, and your shoemakers wouldn't be too pleased either. One-legged punters would be nicking the sample shoes outside the shops and hopping off down the High Street. There would be anarchy.

The Symptoms

Thank God for the free National Health Service, then. This was invented in 1944 by Lord Beveridge, who also devised the recreational drink, by the way. And like the FA Cup it is revered around the world, something Britain does best. However, like any state-run monolith it's got neglectful of giving the punter what he wants. Back in 1944 with doodlebugs buzzing around, Joe Public was deliriously happy if he got a digestive with his cup of tea after the operation. But in the service-led world of the 1990s wholemeal doesn't cut the mustard. People want more out of the NHS or they'll use the competition. And it looks like they are about to get it.

The Diagnosis

Hospitals were invented by monks and nuns – over in Italy they've got establishments that are actually older than St Barts itself, and not just the lifts. They were simple affairs though – a soothing linament and a couple of prayers to the gaffer upstairs and then you pegged it. Things weren't much better in Queen Vic's time: there was Florence Nightingale out in the Crimea and all she could offer our brave boys was a radiant smile and a woolly hat – talk about the Prescription Charge of the Light Brigade! So in the historical perspective your NHS hospital, complete with a matron with the turning circle of HMS *Ark Royal* and Sir James Robertson Justice doing the rounds, was a bit of heaven. Especially if you got a nurse like Shirley Eaton (for those old enough to remember). But the declining standards of the 1970s – Dr Dirk Bogart replaced by Simon Dee, concrete beds causing grief to your nether parts, a tired and repetitive menu that repeated on you, not to mention some miserable little geezer on the hospital radio angling for a job at Radio Caroline – hardly made for a speedy recuperation. Fortunately things are about to change.

The Cure

In our manor the Government have just cut the ribbon on the Hammersmith and Fulham. Eighteen-carat. You could put the word 'Hilton' over the front and people wouldn't notice the difference.

Naturally there were some bolsheviks and luddists who reckoned it was out of order to close two clapped-out, ugly hospitals with bad colour schemes to open this one, but what they don't understand is you can't have everything. Who wouldn't prefer a foyer alive with steel bands, waterfalls, coffee bars, juggling and murals to a bit of red lino and pitted walls painted in War Department stuff, covered in hectoring old posters of lungs like string vests telling you to stop smoking? You'd feel tom-and-dick just walking in there.

So here it is, the hospital of the future. Up until now it has been but a vision in the business portfolio of my imagination. A chain of 'Mr Getwells'. But now, thanks to the charming Veronica Bottomley, it is breeze-blocks, mortar, glass, chrome and concessions. Picture the scene: the porter wheels you in, with a quick pit stop at reception so that the smiling young woman in the blue suit can take a swipe of your plastic, while you pick your menu for dinner and choice of first-run videos. Once the exam and the op are out of the way you're escorted to your suite where there's a low-fat chocolate mint waiting for you on the pillow. If you didn't like the room service menu, there'd be the full range of franchises in the atrium so you could send out for a pizza, southern fried chicken with that unique mix of herbs and spices or a ruby murray if the operation had been particularly gruelling and you'd built up a bit of an appetite. And there'd be none of that 'We'll be there in thirty minutes' malarkey as they'd only need to take a swift ride up the scenic elevator.

Now if you are in the building business I cannot strongly enough recommend a butcher's at the Hammersmith and Fulham. The seasoned eye – from architect to plasterer – won't fail to notice the brilliant forward planning HM's Government demonstrated when they knocked the place up. Change the curtains, upgrade the tellies and it could be one of London's five-star hotels. In the sad event of a slump in the health industry through people living longer etc., the hospital could be transformed with minimum fuss and investment from the far-sighted entrepreneur (modesty forbids) into luxury accommodation for the business traveller and well-heeled tourist. Swap the porter's overall, turn the operating theatres into conference centres or saunas, and you're well on the way to being the next Conrad Hilton, make no mistake.

If you want to see how it's done then go West

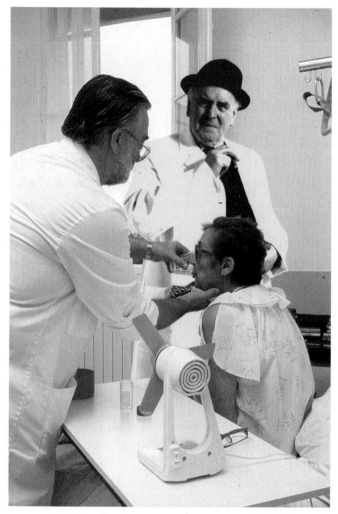

*Care in the Community in action: checking
for possible bed availability, after being
informed by bleeper of an urgent demand
now a business flight to Zurich has been put
back 24 hours.*

up to Hyde Park and clock the Lanesborough. Once a crummy old hospital with no benefit to society, it is now a magnet for both the world's gold card brigade and those who just want to spend the weekend having a laugh at the Queen Mother Gates.

Why can't this work across the country? All a planning authority needs to do is choose desirable sites when they build new hospitals – like old country homes that the Moonies haven't picked up or hectares of our green and pleasant with waterside views – and they would be in the box seat vis-à-vis future developments. The New Forest, the Lake District (Wordsworth country) or the Downs (Marlborough country) would all be perfect locations. And I hear that north of the Watford Gap there are still plenty of workhouses with pleasant south-facing aspects.

GPs on HP

As any of my fellow Wykehamists (customers of the Winchester to you) will confirm: life is a market. Only with that latter-day Lady of the Lamp, Mrs T, did the Government clock this essential truism, roll their sleeves up and dive in, Swiss Army knife clenched in their teeth. Now your local sawbones has got to face it too. And not before time, judging by the amount of Valiums the docs in this neck of the woods have been dishing out to the troubles of all and sundry – you'd think they were Smarties. But now with market forces your local Marcus Welby GP is either going to be a bit more judicious with his prescription pad or he's going to have to use his creative nous to get the necessary pharmaceuticals at wholesale prices. And this of course is where men like myself come in – captains of local industry long experienced in managing the supply and demand game.

Moreover, the average Doctor Kildare might know a verruca from the wrong end of his stethoscope, but does he know how to maximise his resources? Does he know how to release his meagre roll of readies to help the sick and needy? No. But entrepreneurs like myself do. We could develop five-year business plans, advise on investments and mount advertising campaigns for new patients. After all, the more registered bad coughs a practice has, the more financing trickles down from Whitehall. So why not offset the rental on your surgery and the wages for nurses and help with a little incentivising? When some sick little old lady stumbles into the waiting room and takes a number in the queue she could win a nice box of biscuits if hers is the magic ticket. Or be a blood donor and win a holiday for two – the more pints you give, the more exotic the destination! Give a kidney, win a car (specially donated by a superior local firm, naturally). That sort of thing. With the right approach a doctor's surgery could be a hive of creative activity, instead of a mere mausoleum of old magazines.

Post Mortem

To sum up: now that management is wielding the big scalpel the opportunities for real Customer Care in the NHS are unrivalled. Every lung has a silver lining, and there's no reason why having a critical operation should be glum or depressing – now that I've taken the lead, other top business brains will surely get to work to put flesh on the bones of the vision I've eeked out in this chapter. Coming down with something nasty need not be life-threatening. It could be the holiday of a lifetime. And who can say fairer than that?

THE ARTS
Just One Canaletto

Being as how 'Art' is the first three letters of my
name and what I was known by in my Beatnik phase
– come to think of it that's how 'er indoors and I met,
in Toni's Milk Bar down at World's End (it was Toni's
Needle Exchange when I last clapped eyes on it). 'Er's
boat was half obscured by the froth off the top of a
cup of coffee, amazing how Dame Kismet dances on
such pin-heads of happenstance . . .

Anyway, I attach great importance to the Inner
Man and the workings of his imagination, as any
of my bank managers will tell you. But I do like to
know where I stand in matters artistic – as far as I'm
concerned a good painting should have a beginning,
a middle and an end. You'll find many a green-faced
lemon peering out from behind a tree in the Daley
abode. But I also recognise that art must set out
its stall in the commercial market-place if it is to
survive the winter of discontented punters who've
got jack-and-jills to pay.

The getting of grants is therefore of tantamount
importance, and a careful study of the arts sections
of the linens in recent months has given me an inkling

of the fastest access road to the bow-tied brigade's hearts. The 100 per cent cast-iron guaranteed way to get a return on your investment plus a bit of bunce besides used to be bricks and mortar. Now it's bricks and tyres.

In my role of arts entrepreneur I am able to offer budding Michelangelo de Vincis the following concrete carrots to their careers, in return for a token commission and an invite to the opening-night drinkies do down Bond Street:

1. Several gross of Dunlop Radials suitable for attractive mind-stretching sculptures. Many of them are on the bald side, which would achieve a picturesque light-and-shade effect on the underbelly of a dinosaur for example (that was just off the top of my barnet).

2. Several gross of high-quality bricks suitable for dumping in the middle of the Tate and stringing a red rope round. Can be broken if required, the sort of thing which if placed craftily in the exhibit would have the critics coming to blows and affording the young artist some diamond publicity.

Plus I would throw in my own attendance at the interview stage of the Arts Council grant, giving the applicant access to my unrivalled verbals skills, the power of which not a few donkeys missing their hind legs will attest to.

My other artistic venture whose doors are expected

When I heard that the Great and the Good were descending on the Serpentine Gallery in their posh Georgio Army-and-Navy suits for a butcher's at a dead sheep that some bright spark had stuck in a jar of gherkins, I sensed a window of opportunity being slid open round the back of my gaff.

Visitors to Planet Cricklewood will from now on be able to feast their minces on the Daley Pickled Shark. I feel that this sculpture makes a valuable statement on both man's inhumanity to man and the futility of war (the tuna variety). And at only 25K – not including tank – it's an absolute steal!

to open to the hoypaloy in early 1995 is Planet Cricklewood, a filling station and themed eaterie near Staples Corner and thus handy for the carriage trade on their way Up West. This came about when my boy was driving me past a skip parked outside Elstree Studios and I spotted that it was piled high with memorabilias from the great days of the British cinema, when U-boat commanders panicked at the sight of Jack Hawkins in a duffle coat and James Bond defeated the Red Menace with a blow from a poisoned toe-cap.

All items will be on sale at competitive prices, and punters will be informed that a proportion of each sum will be donated towards the revival of the film industry. At this moment in time I am negotiating with some Ivory Merchant geezers who say they want to siphon their profits from the elephant trade into making films 'reflecting the peculiar character of the English way of life'. I couldn't agree more with their aims and I've got a working title for our first venture already: *Arthur 3*.

OUR NATIONAL HERITAGE
The Chipboard Jungle

Ever since the Romans started the immigration ball rolling, bringing with them their constant hot water and two-car garages, this little nation of ours has been a mecca for all those visionary entrepreneurs who dabbled in the bricks and mortar game. Whether it was a des-res made out of turf, bijou caves (suit first-time hermit) or the Gorbals, we Brits have always embraced a bit of variety and a touch of the eccentric when it came to the family pile. Of course we've also managed to maintain our traditional healthy reserve and sceptical view of dodgy foreign practice. And a good thing too, I hear you say – otherwise we'd have been having hot baths two thousand years ago, and then where would we be? Not to mention the bidet, that hip bath with the barmy French plumbing.

There's no getting away from it, on the old heritage dartboard this fair isle used to score a big one hundred and eighty. Buck House, Leeds Castle, the Cutty Sark – every year scores of frenzied foreigners poured through Heathrow and Dover with their Nikon One-Touches, eager to capture their own little bit of Blighty. Some even brought camcorders, hoping to spot a hotel sliding down a cliff. And that's because Christopher Wren, Capability Brown and Van Der Valk had all done a handsome job turning the United Kingdom into an architectural cul-de-sac. Your multi-coloured trippers could roam round the classical gardens, gawp at pictures of geezers in floppy hats, hope to get a butcher's at Helen Bonhoma Cartier, stick a naughty foot on the other side of the rope marked 'Strictly Private' then shell out a pony for a cream tea. Everybody knew their place.

Now though, all we bung up are concrete cows and Meccano monstrosities with not only the drainpipes on the outside but all the plumbing as well. It makes me want to weep. I can't see your Japanese industrialist taking his one week's holiday in fifty years to fly in and have a dekko at some prefab with a plywood extension. And how many Texan billionaires are going to buckle into Concorde delirious in the knowledge that they're a few hours from communing with some office block that looks like a wireless? Not a lot, as that follically-challenged conjuror puts it.

What has happened to our sense of values, our desire to create something that'll last beyond the next Big Wind? Ours is a society that has become happy to grab what it can now, and to hell with the hinterland. Luckily there's a ray, indeed an Arthur of hope, a friendly St Bernard heading straight for the moral snowdrift with a barrel of 100 per cent proof sound advice hanging round his chops.

As a bit of a landed gent myself with several properties to my name – all in knockout postal codes – I am doing my little bit to stem the tide of dull modernity: central heating, double glazing, that sort of frippery. While I am more than happy to be called upon by my friends the tenants to sort the odd leak here and structural hitch there, I have to say to them: tradition is a double-edged sword. You get to live in a listed building with rococo kitchen and baroque bathroom but by the same token you've got to look a bit sharpish in case the ceiling pays an unexpected visit on your quarry tiles. I'm no hands-off landlord, I need hardly tell you – I'm more the Loco Parent sort, at the sharp end of a call for traditional British values to reassert themselves. Do you think them four-storey gaffs were built for a yuppie couple with a BMW outside and a cheese plant and two chairs made out of pipe-cleaners in the front room? No. They was teeming. Your Victorian nuclear family had more kids than the Osmonds, that bunch of crooners from the Mormon housing estate. Then there was the help downstairs and a couple of old ladies knocking up T-shirts in the attic. This wasn't just a house, it was a community.

So when some chisel-faced Stalinist comes round from the town hall to accuse me of exploitation, I point out, oh country air, that I happen to be upholding one of the last remaining slices of British heritage. All of us pitching in together – a touch of the Dunkirk spirit, everybody out and all that. Just like in the Blitz. 'In more ways than one,' this little Hitler reincarnate snaps, his row of ball pens quivering indignantly in his top pocket, 'Mr Daley, your properties are Rackman-esque.'

'It's no use showing off that you know American writers,' I reply, 'I only read home-grown. And anyway, what could be more British than a score of punters enduring hardship so that the captains of industry can show a nice little profit at the end of the week? Haven't you heard of privatisation?'

But it all set me thinking about what more I could do to repel the imposition of concrete carbuncles upon manors up and down the land. And it was watching Windsor Castle light up the night sky that gave my imagination the spark it needed – a cruel twist of fate that I am sure Her Majesty would have the magnanimosity to treat as a trifle, especially now that I've given her a leg-up with her Christmas message (see page 19).

We were down the Winchester when it happened. Dave, myself and a few of the regulars were gathered round admiring a brand new colour telly (it had even got the polystyrene packing and the little packet of sand) which I'd sold Dave for the knock-down price of a couple of centuries. When whoosh. Up goes Windsor.

'Isn't that awful,' I said. 'It looks just like old Bernie the Bolt's DIY warehouse when that went up.'

'Blimey Arthur, it's almost as if the fire's actually coming out of the telly,' Dave said.

'Well that's the magic of it, see. The picture is so clear you think you can smell smoke. State of the art, Dave.'

'Arthur, the TV *is* on fire,' Dave pointed out.

When we'd mopped up and tried for half an hour to get the picture back, Dave, rather churlishly I thought, demanded the return of his ackers.

'Dave – I robbed myself to sell you that telly. Up West punters are shelling out five hundred nicker for a set a quarter the size of this. It's got all the latest oriental cutting-edge technology. As the Bard says, Dave . . .'

'As Dave says – *you're* barred,' he retorted, quick as a flash. Come to think of it, the shock he got off the telly when he was standing in that puddle of water must have re-activated a long-dormant sense of humour. Maybe there is something in that Jurassic Park malarkey.

Anyway, by now my mind was grazing on pastures new. Mention of the Great Fire of Windsor and Bernie's gaff in the same breath had given me an idea next to which anything Archimedes came up with was a drop in the ocean. As the Bard *did* say:

dreams are made of this stuff.

Trouble, my old Mum used to say, always comes in threes, like the Number 11 bus. And that certainly happened for Bernie the Bolt, who acquired said moniker on account of his prodigious ability to turn Scotch mist whenever the long arm in blue made an appearance in the vicinity of his genuine Raich Cartier watches and perfume stall. Anyway, back in the booming Eighties you couldn't swing a spirit level in old Bernie's DIY warehouse for the barbour and velvet headband brigade, force-feeding their Volvos with trellises, topiaries, apiaries, steamers, sanders and matt vinyl finish in subtle shades of white. Come the recession though, it was like the Oval on a Tuesday all year round. The place was gobi. Bernie had to flog his hacienda down the Algarve. His trouble gave him serious grief over the shortfall in her spending money. And no more celebrity golf with Tarby, Lynchy and half of the Two Ronnies. By 1990 Bernie was feeling a bit embarrassed on the cash-flow front on account of none flowing in and a bucketload pouring out. His back was well and truly up against the plasterboard.

Now, I always look out for a friend in need, so I whispered into Bernie's shell-like (conch shell, that is – Bernie's never been much of an oil painting) the three little words that my bumps told me might get him out of the molasses he was in. Diversification.

'Bernie,' I told him, 'punters may not be laying out the folding stuff for home improvements, but everyone needs a laugh, especially in times as troubled as ours, with Mogadon Man at Number 10 presiding over a bunch of indiscriminate wick-dippers.' Bernie got my gist in a trice and agreed to take two gross of best Chinese fireworks off my hands. November 5th was looming on the horizon and knowing Bernie's connections with the men in aprons and the swift handshake I felt sure he could arrange to supply Fulham with all the bangers and rockets they needed. It'll be just like the Silver Jubilee all over again, I told him, that golden summer of 1977 when Ginny Wade beat that Dutch lemon with the bandaged leg.

What happened next was like some Orvillian nightmare. With the fireworks safely locked up in Bernie's paint and plywood palace the world was smelling roses. Bernie had put an advance my way with the balance due when the local authority dug into its slush fund. Then by some cruel twist of nature the fireworks spontaneously combusted and Bernie's warehouse looked like something out of one of them Arnold Schickelgruber movies. Luckily for Bernie he was insured. Unluckily for me his insurance company said my Chinese fireworks was about as stable as the Hindenburg.

Now of course this was a diabolical slur. The Chinese is to fireworks what Britain is to tea. Does

anyone go to the U. of S. A. and say their hamburg-
ers are off-colour? Or tell the French their frogs legs
have got gout? Yet here's some Nimrod from the Pru
not only hurling a monkey wrench into the first green
shoots of economic recovery but casting nasturtiums
about our Asian cousins' ability to make a sparkler.
When he pointed out that the Chinese fireworks were
from North Korea as it happened, I realised what a
low ebb the tide of River Knowledge had reached.
As I explained to him, if you buy a Japanese TV and
it says 'Made in Wales' on it, you don't say this isn't
a Japanese telly it's a Taff telly. We're all one nation
now, Pacific rim, everyone famous for fifteen minutes.
Next, I said, you'll be telling me Scotland isn't part of
England. That shut him up.

Still out of pocket on the deal, I heard it from
the Grapevine (a boozer up West that's twinned with
the Winchester) that Bernie had been seen wassailing
with a healthy wedge of readies always to hand. I was
determined to have it out with him and was all set
to send my minder round for a one-on-one discussion
when the news came through that Bernie had been
nicked for insurance fraud. It seems my fireworks
went off with a little help from a blowtorch!

'Now this is all very interesting social history,
Arthur,' you're no doubt saying, 'but how does your
misfortune at the hands of the nefarious The Bolt
lead to a culturally uplifting experience guaranteed

to put Britain's proud architectural heritage back in the sightseer's global A-to-Z?' Like this. When the idea came to me it was like the M25 on rush hour: wallop. A serious Damascus moment. What was the top-of-the-bill excursion for Johnny Foreign Tourist? Windsor. And wouldn't it be nice if they all had some souvenir to take home and stick on the mantelpiece in their mud huts, apart from plastic beefeater dolls and rubber plods' helmets?

As the man from Del Monte might say: yes. But could I get hold of any actual burnt offerings from Windsor Castle? No I could not. Didn't anyone in authority in this country have any vision, any pride? Again, negatory. Had Maggie still been in charge I reckon you'd have seen best bids going in for any blackened heirlooms or at any rate a decent fire sale. But while I couldn't get my mits on authentic Windsor timbers, I had no difficulty shifting Bernie the Bolt's charred pine and two-by-four round the lock-up. After all, I was well out of pocket on account of his own DIY activities. An axe and some labels and I was the proud possessor of five thousand pieces of genuine Windsor Castle. Or at any rate a singed copy. At a fiver a pop the whole deal was looking very handsome.

After my first day's trading up by the Tower of London I was nearly a grand to the better. Tired but happy, as I used to write in my school essays,

I repaired to the Winchester for a well-earned VAT and explained to Dave the highly patriotic nature of my endeavours.

'You have in your hand, Dave, the sacred remains of a cherished British landmark.'

'It looks like a bit of Bernie the Bolt's fire damaged two-by-four to me.'

'Dave! Please! Up till the other day this historic plank was keeping the elements off our dear Queen's bonce. Two-by-four? This isn't just Windsor Castle, Dave. This is heritage. Agincourt. Shakespeare. Geoff Hurst at Wembley. Nigel Mansell. Pearl and Dean.' I was hitting my stride. 'These sticks are a time machine back to an England of fair play, knights on snortin' steeds, noblesse oblige and chivas regal. All their lives the jabbering alien hordes have fantasies about coming to Britain – and when they get here, what do they find? Pasta, lager and Alsatian kebabs. I'm giving them tradition. Hold the dream. The eternal flame, all that.'

'What are you going to do next, Arthur?' asked my boy, sticking an inappropriate oar in as per usual. 'Sell bits of house-brick and claim it's Stonehenge? Or what about roof slate? You could say that was York Minster!'

I put on my best air of injured dignity, while making a mental note of the roof slate idea. 'Gentlemen, please, to coin a phrase – when Dame Opportunity knocks, you open the door and pull up a chair for her.' It was at this moment that there was a peremptory knock on the Winchester's outer casement, and the drawbridge was lowered to reveal a grim reaper from the Met, clutching a piece of my wood, or as it said on the label, 'Genuine Windsor timber tortured by the flames that made a Nation mourn. £5 o.n.o.'

'Daley,' he began, with a curl of the lip you could roll Rizlas up in, 'I suppose you wouldn't know anything about some stolen evidence from Bernie the Bolt's insurance fraud? Nor how said wood turned up in several popular tourist spots masquerading as the property of the Crown?'

He must have thought he'd got me needing snookers, but cometh the hour cometh the man, as some geezer with a lisp once said.

'Thank God, Sergeant!' I cried, 'You've managed to save some too! If you go to my lock-up you'll find many more pieces like it. As a patriot I felt it my solemn duty to try and salvage as much of Windsor Castle as possible from the grip of spivs and black-marketeers before it left our shores forever and suffered the fate of the *Queen Mary*, turned into a third-rate boarding house. Now you tell me they're not kosher. Let me tell you, Sergeant – the out-of-pocket experience I am suffering is as nothing to the joy I feel that the Castle hasn't gone the same way as British Rail, broken up for the fiscal gain of hucksters. Here's a health unto Her Majesty!' I finished, draining my VAT and pushing the empty glass in his direction.

` 'You'll be telling me you're getting the OBE next,' growled the gutted plod.

'And I distinctly put an X for No Publicity,' I countered, wiping my feet on him. 'Suffice it to me to remind you of the words of Ludovic Kennedy – "Ask not what your country can do for you, but what you can do for your country".'

THIS SPORTING LIFE

There is hardly a sport known to man that hasn't been given to the world by us Brits. Back in the eighteenth century when the Frog monarchy was putting its neck on the line for the right to eat cake, they were getting the light roller out at Hampstead Heath and practising their forward defensive. And ever since then plucky little bands of colonials and that surly bunch of unshaven convicts from Down Under have been queueing up for the privilege of being put to the sword by the finest and brightest of England's young men: Lord Ted, Sir Geoffrey, Compo and Foggy.

Twas ever thusly: even though the eternal flame of the Olympics was lit originally by some ancient Phil the Greek, need I remind you who supplied the Lucozade and Mars Bars? And then in the 1920s of course it was us who well and truly showed the Bubbles how a race should be run, when our boys Harold Abrahams and Colin Welland turned it into a procession, leaving an assortment of souped-up Chinamen and war criminals floundering in slow-motion behind them before the clock had even struck one.

But what's the situation now? Seb Coe's decided to follow in the plimmies of the great Christopher Chatterley and run for Parliament instead, leaving the flag to be waved by a bunch of YTS lads whipped off a street corner south of the River, all body-hugging Lycra and a butcher's at the orchestrals for the ladies. And as for cricket: talk about 'Produce of More than One Country'! We pack the side with Smithy and Hicky and other benefit-claimers and we *still* can't even beat Sri Lon or whatever it calls itself these days. I won't even mention our national game – except to say that the team was never going to get anywhere while it was being managed by somebody who thought tactics is a packet of mints. Luckily the poisoned cello has now been handed to a real visionary, who knows how to handle toffs and touts alike. My old friend Tel deserves a chapter to himself (just to list his companies and pubs) and I like to think it was me putting my point of view forcibly in the vicinity of the Directors' Box at the Cottage that led to the Powers What Be putting their specs on and making a far-sighted appointment.

Because let's face it, pretty soon the only sports left that show off our unique talent for combining the Corinthian ideal and supreme physical fitness will be snooker and darts. Not that I'm maligning either of these two excellent pastimes: a finer body of men you won't meet east of the Rio, Dalston. It's just that, as a true patriot I happen to believe that when it comes to working it up the foreigners, the Battle of Waterloo is won on the level playing fields of Eton, rather than the Winchester.

So the starter for ten is: how do we get the nation back into pole sporting position, when 'UK Gold' means more than just a lot of duff old TV shows full of geezers in kipper ties? Let's just think back to Napoleon for a minute. What else was he famous for, apart from always keeping his hand on his wallet so's Josephine (or 'Er in the Tent) couldn't make off round the Paris fashion houses with his hard-earned sous? That's right: calling us 'A nation of shopkeepers'. And here – as the England physio says to Gazza when he limps off the field with a chipped fingernail – is the rub.

Getting A Result

It's my bone of contention that sport needs some proper attention at the grass-roots or Astroturf level. Proper funding. Because let's face it, the days of kids honing their skills on the park by kicking a ball between two piles of jumpers are long gone. Now they'd turn their backs on the goal for an instant to form a defensive wall and the jumpers'd be off getting a respray. The need for decent facilities to nurture the next Virginia Wade or David Gowie is sore, and can best be summed up in a phrase every budding entrepreneur should have hanging above his bed:

IF YOU CAN'T BEAT 'EM, SPONSOR 'EM

What do you see when the England cricket team puffs its way out onto the pitch at Lord's, or the average Brit tennis player strides confidently onto the court at Wimbledon preceded by guide dog? I know what I see: acres of virgin white flannel and terylene, that's what. Now look at the catchment area of the two venues – a riot of private hospitals, take-away ruby houses and quality-used-motor sales executives less than a stone's away, all vying for custom. But where are the ads? Each shirt as far as I'm concerned could be a designated development area. A tasteful commercial emblazoned across each English breast and thigh would bring much-needed mazuma into the game. Make the ball harder to spot for the opposition, an' all.

I wrote to the soccer authorities on this very subject last year when it became obvious that our lads had less chance of qualifying for the 1994 World Cup than that baldy Taff lefty Neil Kojak had of becoming Prime Minister. I was keen to promote the interests of Daley Motors across the pond and thought, where better than the shirt of the Brit referee – the governing body FAFF decrees that there always has to be one,

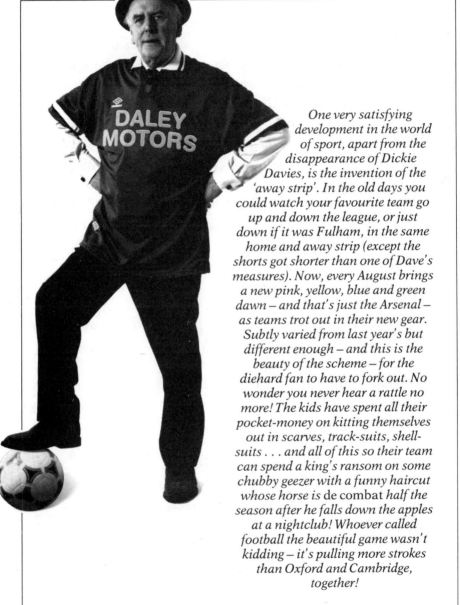

One very satisfying development in the world of sport, apart from the disappearance of Dickie Davies, is the invention of the 'away strip'. In the old days you could watch your favourite team go up and down the league, or just down if it was Fulham, in the same home and away strip (except the shorts got shorter than one of Dave's measures). Now, every August brings a new pink, yellow, blue and green dawn – and that's just the Arsenal – as teams trot out in their new gear. Subtly varied from last year's but different enough – and this is the beauty of the scheme – for the diehard fan to have to fork out. No wonder you never hear a rattle no more! The kids have spent all their pocket-money on kitting themselves out in scarves, track-suits, shell-suits . . . and all of this so their team can spend a king's ransom on some chubby geezer with a funny haircut whose horse is de combat half the season after he falls down the apples at a nightclub! Whoever called football the beautiful game wasn't kidding – it's pulling more strokes than Oxford and Cambridge, together!

141

something for the tourists to go and cheer on in loo of an actual team: remember Jack Taylor, the pork butcher from Wolverhampton, who reminded West Germany who won the war by awarding a penalty against them in the first minute of the 1974 Final? And what reaction did I get from the FA? Stick 'Sweet' in front of it and you'd be on the warm side. Typical. But there you are: like it says in the Bible, we men of honour are often without profit in our own country. It reminds me of what happened the last time I tried to set up a fight (that's right, I used to be at the sharp end of the promotion business: who do you think gave Barry Hernia his name and sent Don King's hair the way it is?).

I was all set to give my boy the big speech about 'You could be a contender' but his guard was up.

'I don't wanna know.'

'Have you had a better offer?' I countered. 'One-night stand on the door at a disco? Is your diary full? I'm offering you dignity, respect . . .'

'Are you kidding?' (Below the belt, that.)

'All right – money.' I hit him with a right, and followed with a double whammy. 'Money which you are severely deficient of at this moment in time. Like your brethren who've frittered away their wealth, boozing all night, business ventures with no chance, fair-weather friends who didn't have an umbrella between them.' (Jab, jab, jab.) 'In the immortal words of Willy Pep: "First you lose your legs and then you lose your friends".'

He thought he'd got me on the ropes when he asked where this so-called money was going to come from. But I was ready, and moved in for the kill. The jackpot, three lemons all in a row.

'Sponsorship – I'll take your dressing-gown to Nick the Cleaner. He'll love it. Two-Hour Service, Alterations Our Speciality, Try Our New Luxury Shirt Service ... stick "The Winchester" on the bum of your trunks and you're a walking industry.'

As I remember, I'd have been better off putting 'Smirnoff' and 'Schweppes' on the soles of his shoes, but that's not the point ...

Tunes of Glory

It won't have escaped your attention that the only thing the England World Cup Squad has been half-way decent at since the days of Sir Alf Ramsey and Nobby Stiles brandishing his hampsteads, is in getting their Official Song to the top of the hit parade. Once again last year, in the dark days after we didn't qualify, I was prepared to do my bit in the national interest: it was obvious that what was needed was an uplifting ditty that would take everyone's minds off their woes, and have Postman Pat whistling of a morning as he shoved the old Mad Max demands in through the letter-box (not mine, of course, see page 77).

With this in mind, I submitted the following lyrics to the relevant authorities, adding a crocodile to the effect that of course now the England lads weren't going, I'd be happy to supply them with sponsored transportation as they went about their off-duty business in Greater London, whether it be cutting the ribbon to open a new Asda in Gants Hill or cutting the rug in Mr Bojangles, Perivale.

Daley Motors – that's what we drive in town.
Arthur Daley, he'll never
Let You Down.
Every Motor is fully guaranteed,
Yes that's right, an Arthur Daley Motor's what you need!

Catchy, I thought – and clever too: crossword buffs will already have spotted the acrylic that spells out a certain name from the first letters. I never heard back, though.

The Sport of Kings (or A Daley at the Races)

But then we've never known how to handle our sports superstars properly. I'll give you another for-instance: remember that time Desert Orchid went down with a spot of lurgi? The nation held its breath, sackloads of get-well cards outside the stable door, special prayers said in the private chapel at Windsor. Dessie came through with flying colours, minus ten feet of his small intestine. End of story.

Yet here's me with ready-made space in the lock-up and a built-in marketing operation, panting for the stalls to open so's I can offer the public a once-in-a-lifetime opportunity:

> **We all know**
> **DESSIE'S**
> **got**
> **GUTS!**
> **Now here's**
> **your chance**
> **to own**
> **a**
> **bit of them!!**

Simple, isn't it. But like ring-pulls on dog food, all the best ideas are. I reckoned ten feet of intestine, that's 120 inches, 240 pieces cut sideways, pin 'em to a varnished piece of four-by-two, pony a time if you'll pardon the expression, that's six grand before deductions and a monkey bunged to the League Against Cruelty to Horses for promotional purposes. And that's only for the genuine bits: Dave's got some very good contacts in the pub sausage trade who I know get stuck with a lot of leftovers . . .

But I regress. What I'm saying is that the world of sport offers a whole window of opportunities that the average punter is ready and willing to clamber through and part with his hard-earned rather than frittering it away on double-glazing if you follow my drift. This came home to me the other evening when I was sitting there with 'er indoors in front of our visual entertainments multi-channel complex, sampling what was on offer. As it happens there was no choice: since 'er sat on the remote the picture's stuck between what's on and what's on Teletext, and that bloke in the corner doing the deaf-and-dumb signals doesn't help either. Anyway, in the confusion I managed to pick out an 0891 number which promised a horse running the next day that would win doing handsprings, with its head in its chest, shelling peas, etc. Being in a Royal Navy situation (in need of a sub) I waited till 'er had climbed the wooden hill to

Bedfordshire, got on the dog and rang the number. Ten minutes and five quid later they'd given me the name of an odds-on favourite.

Eroica! My mind went to work as fast as a French train before it gets to our end of the Channel Tunnel, and next day in the motor I outlined the plan to my boy.

'Listen – we put an ad in the *Sporting Life*. We get three telephones. We don't ask for money. No fees from the clients. They phone us and we give them three horses. All we ask is this: if you bet, put on ten pounds for us. And if they win then send us a cheque. That's our commission.'

'They'd have to be barmy,' he replied, loyal as ever.

'Don't you believe in trust? The commercial world is based on trust, don't you realise that? That's the system. You pay your debts. You work for a factory and they give you your wages at the end of the week . . .'

'Who's this "you" you're talking about?'

'Never mind that,' I said. 'The issue of the moment is trust. We're selling an advisory service to our clients. We're consultants.'

'Let me get this right,' he says, trying the patience of Oddjob as we drove to the nerve centre of my operation. 'I pick up the phone and give the geezer three horses in different races, and remind him to put a tenner on for us. Next guy phones and I give three other names. Then the next guy gets three other horses and then I go back to the first three when somebody else phones. Right?'

I was proud of him. 'This is a great opportunity for you,' I said. 'You're always going on about improving yourself. Now you've got an office job. Receptionist-cum-manager. A bit of responsibility.'

'Where is the office?' he asked.

I stopped the car and pointed across the street.

'You mean I've got to mind THREE PUBLIC TELE-PHONES?!? I'll be nicked!'

' 'Course you won't,' I said. 'They're ours. Look at the stickers: *"Out Of Order".'*

'You're out of order, Arthur,' he snapped, made an excuse and left. I don't know, the youth of today never think positive.

Say what you like about our sporting decline though: we still lead the world in Diving. Not to mention Ducking.

A MAN FOR ALL NEXT SEASON
Terry Venables

Every loyal Englishman with the blood of Henry the Fifth, Isaac Newton and Gerald Ratner coursing through his veins remembers where he was on 23 November 1993. I was in the Winchester as it happens, there being a Y in the day, and Dave's beer flowed like water – for some reason he gets very sensitive when you say that – at the news that the Great Begetter of Woes, the man some pundits had likened to a root vegetable, had decided to quit the battlefield of our national pastime and ply his trade in the Sherpa Diaspora Gaffs League or whatever it's called, with a couple of 5-watt floodlights and a steep hill from the away end. Yes, Graham Taylor had resigned.

We were a country sore afflicted, as it says in the Gideon Bible I always carry around with me. The lack of need to apply for an American visa this year had left John Bull slumped in his armchair, stunned mute and babbling with his lean cuisine getting cold and his lager getting warm as he'd watched our boys take a right pasting from a bunch of trolls from Norway and Polish refugees with bad haircuts.

But out of the ashes of our World Cup defeats has come new hope. Terry Venables is the new England manager. Up and down the land ticker tape has flown out of windows as we see a man to admire take up the cudgel and the long stud. I myself am proud to have met him. It was an evening down the Palais in the 1970s (I remember because I took 'er indoors out), devoted to popular favourites and football anecdotes as crooned and recited by the young Tel, and I must say he had a very nice singing voice. No doubt about it, the lad was eighteen-carat. No, I think I'd revise that and say twenty-two-carat. Stand on me.

There can be no question that Terry Vegetables has got the form for the job, compared to his predecessor who frankly was a couple of oranges short at half-time in the managerial department. With years of experience at the helm of one of this country's great cruise liners of industry, I can spot a winner. I mean, Dave handles a bar very nicely but I wouldn't put him in charge of Whitbreads, if you take my meaning. Not even their horses.

Tel's talents were apparent at Tottenham Hotspur, where he showed his deep understanding of the psychological niceties of the game by introducing an eye-catching new line of merchandise. Always a sharp dresser himself, he realised the advantages to be gained by kitting the lads out in big European-style shorts for the FA Cup Final, which left Cloughie's mob looking very redundant coal-pit and out of it. In fact Cloughie was *really* out of it after disappearing up the tunnel for a quick VAT at full-time! He took one look at the natty Londoners and realised the game was up.

I feel sure we can expect to see this kind of unique thinking now that Terry's the England supremo. Never to be seen without a whistle on himself, I'm sure he knows a couple of outfitters who can knock up the squad's clobber at a keen price, new kit every game. Graham Taylor, deranged by fear, always forgot his threads and had to sit around in someone's borrowed tracksuit. Not at all seemly – I can only guess what Sir Bert Millichip, Sir Alf Ramsey and Sir John Gielgud thought of things when they tuned into Sky to watch the game.

What is more, Terry is bound to keep the fans happy with his total football philosophy. He can coach the side and arrange the charter flights to Milan and produce the new scarves and the little mini-footballs, do a TV commentary and get the players a nice Italian dinner at a competitive price. And if the lads get a bit restless on the bus he can dish out copies of his Hazell novels. Those Chelsea pensioners down the FA don't know how lucky they are. They've got the dream ticket and it's all in one Renault Espace Man. Talking of tickets, my idea (faxed through to Tel the minute I heard about his appointment) of setting up a bucket shop round the back of Scratchwood Services on the M1 is one of many far-sighted ventures which can only benefit disadvantaged Scouse punters, who would otherwise be polluting the leafy lanes of Wembley with their guttural animal cries.

Terry is also a man after my own heart with his considerable interest in an exclusive drinking club, up Kensington way. I think that speaks volumes. Your average slowing-up footballer looks forward to managing some country pub or opening a sports shop in Merton. Few have the vision to deck out the basement of an old department store, transforming it into a cosy snug for *bon mots*, heady debate and a distinctive house white – not to mention furnishing the place with beer-mats and ashtrays worth a few hundred grand of anybody's money. Imagine what Terry could do down the Great White Way!

Yes, vision – that's what I'm talking about. Mark my words, Terry Venables will join the panther of great names and see Blighty right, or I'm not a car dealer with thirty years' trouble-free sales behind me. I can feel it in my water – a regular Mister 115 Per Cent, before the service charge . . . Terry is one of our own.

TRANSPORT
Up the Junction

As we embark on the penultimate lap before the birth of the new millinerium, one of the most pressing concerns up and down the land is how we get about. It's all very well for Raymond Baxter and Murray Walker to be talking about Information Superhighways – but has the M11 got a service station yet? And how many more lanes are they going to stick on the M25? Soon it'll be so big we'll be able to see the motors chugging round in circles from the vantage point of the Winchester . . . and then a pedestrian tunnel to the bar itself can only be a step away! Any road up (and they usually are), imagine trying to change lane if there's fourteen to choose from. At the moment, on the few occasions that necessitate my venturing off my home turf, I can be cruising along in the fast lane, notice that the turn-off to Heathrow is imminent, give a quick tug to the Jag's power-assisted and be cosy on the left-hand side in a trice.

Which reminds me – one's fellow citizens all respect a Jag. Wherever I go and am negotiating said manoeuvre, other drivers flash their lights and wave their arms about as a form of salute. Now that's something you don't hear about in the official brochure but could be highly pertinent to any future vehicle purchase, indeed worth a couple of extra ponies on the asking price. Which reminds me again. I do actually happen to have a brace of classic Jags on the forecourt that are begging for a good home. Like anything vintage, they just get better and better with age. If Inspector Morse himself had been pulling down a Chief Super's wedge and not spending all his green folding on the works of Mozart and Stromboli he'd probably have bagged the pair, one for himself and one for his oily rag.

But I'm off on a B-road again. Let's get back to changing lanes, a nifty bit of footwork on my part as it stands, which would have all the priests flocking to the window in a motor ad. Not to mention Nicole panting to give me her phone number. But imagine if I'm cruising along in a seven-lane motorway. I've got no hope of banking over for my turn-off. Salesmen from across the land are going to get onto the M25 and never get off – not even at the South Mimms Happy Chef for a much-needed Early Starter breakfast and the possibility of bumping into our Great Leader as he butters a piece of bread that's been wafted in the vague vicinity of a toaster. Gleaming skeletons these reps'll be, with their drip-dry shirts hanging unworn on the hooks behind their heads in silent mockery. Dutch lorries full of tulips and Spanish truckloads of water melons are never going to get to market, they'll just be circling round till they pass their sell-by date, like those bits of old Sputniks forever whizzing round the stratosphere.

Now there's a thought for economic regeneration! While our European cousins are cursing the traffic cones and chomping on their triangular Swiss Yorkie bars, loyal Brit hauliers with traditional tattoos can duck and dive down the backroads, Garfields swinging in the breeze, and deliver good old British and Commonwealth chattels to anxious storekeepers. So for once the Government was coming clean when they said motorways will help the economy. They could build twenty-five lane motorways up and down and across the country simply to keep the hordes of Euro-imports at bay. A German loaded up with shavers destined for Lincoln could alight at Harwich and not be heard of again till he got to the Outer Hebrides, where they all cultivate beards. There would be mayhem, from which the canny British entrepreneur and therefore the country as a whole could only but benefit.

Another useful weapon in this trade battle would be road signs. During the last conflict dodgy signs were stuck up everywhere to confuse potential invaders and fifth columnists out canvassing for the Labour Party. Well, as every motorist will tell you, the tradition lives on to this very day. Wherever you go there are plentiful road signs, thus lulling you into a false sense of security – until a critical point about ten miles from your destination, when they are completely hidden behind a tree that was just a sapling when the sign was built ... or else they vanish completely. I can just see some Viking Rubber Duck with an artic full of bacon doing his nut, while a British farmer with his truckload of porkers sneaks to market first. Everyone needs a competitive edge, and I think you'd have to agree a little Bank Holiday chaos is a small price to pay for putting Britain back on four wheels and in pole position.

A Road to Nowhere

As we all know, the Romans brought roads with them, building cities where they took a rest for the night until they got to Scotland, where they took one look and built a wall instead. Either that or they built them in straight lines to places where nobody wanted to go, like Wales. For years afterwards medieval punters were crowded into smelly cramped stage-coaches full of kids being tom-and-dick that took days to get anywhere, so your leather purse had the added stress of a night in an half-timbered Thistle Forte (derived from the Latin, meaning you need your strength). And they didn't have trouser-presses or complimentary tubs of VHS milk in those days, either. Then you'd be jammed back on the stage and

*Besides Adrian and his Wall, the Romans
also gave us the first toll bridges, as this
ancient coin recently discovered in the mud
near Southwark demonstrates. Experts
believe they were invented after a
disagreement between a centurion and an
Anglo-Saxon hackney cart driver, who
wouldn't take him south of the river after
midnight as this meant finding the source of
the Thames in leafy Bucks when the driver
wanted to get home to Essex. The lynx-eyed
may spot the Latin words-to-the-wise 'Caveat
Emptor' encircling the noble Roman's bonce.*

in the hands of some lunatic driver who didn't know Newgate from Aldgate, and you'd career round the country for another eight hours without so much as the whiff of a ham bap. And he'd expect a silver collection.

Then came the railways. Old Robert Louis Stevenson took a bit of time off from writing Dr Jekyll and Douglas Hurd to invent his rocket train, the prototype with a big funnel of that orange contraption the French are always banging on about, the TSB. Trains went everywhere, and everyone worth his salt had their own train company. That's why even today the Queen has a Royal Train which she's prepared to let out to the younger element for a bit of how's-one's-father (see also page 19). It was still too early for the public to stand them a customised Phantom V or a yacht, so old Queen Vic shelled out for a train. Then of course she actually wanted to be able to go to Balmoral and Sandringham and Centre Parc on it, so the British Navvy started building a bucketload of tracks, thus for the first and last time in our history creating full employment.

These were the great times. Britain bestrode the oceans. John Bull's breast swelled with confidence, his doughty heart thumping with eternal hope. Kids were given grandiose monikers like Isambard Kingdom Brunel and Capability Brown and Knight Frank Rutley. Half the countries in the world were painted pink and those that weren't wanted to be, and they all had trains and timetables that weren't just put up to give frustrated passengers a laugh while they waited at Fenchurch Street. No one had heard of Dr Beeching or Network North by North-west Railtrack plc. But now look where we are. Gridlock. Walking along tunnels. Doors bursting open. Where – I ask you – has public transport got us?

But times they are a-changing as Dylan Thomas said before he'd had a skinful. Thanks to a modicum of foresight by Mr Magoo at Number 10 – not to mention revenge for being turned down for a bus conductor's job – the days of public transport will soon be over. Soon there'll be forty-eight different train companies, and if you want to get anywhere by tomorrow you'll have to sling your hook continentally. Your Euro-traveller in his beige mac with the collar up might be able to go from Paris to Berlin while having half an hour's kip in a baguette, but once within sight of the White Cliffs they'll learn to do things our way. Halfway through the Channel Tunnel and the edges of the sandwiches will start curling up as if by magic. The fizzy water'll go flat and warm, and the fruitcake'll be all that's left on the delicatessen counter.

You see, history has taught us that going places fast has got us nowhere. Remember the Blue Streak? I thought not, it's confined to the backwaters of telly quiz programmes like the Ronco Buttoneer. So just like the Victorians did, we're going to take our time and re-emerge a greater nation because of it. How's that, you might wonder? Well let's just look at railway catering as a classic example. If your punter can hurtle between European capitals in two shakes of the cat's proverbials, then he's not going to spend his hard earned ecus on meals on board, he'll hang on for a sausage and sauerkraut when he gets there. But the slower your train goes as it plods round the Ashford loop the more hot bacon and tomato rolls and McEwans Export you're going to flog. *Sine cure non* I think you'll agree. A much tidier result. (See page 86 for the next leg of the Euro-journey.)

And what can beat the freedom of the road? The enterprise culture needs to be freed of the meddlings of petty bureaucracy in order to express itself. And it's the same when you're in the jam jar. The Briton in his motor is just like the Roman in his chariot – apart from the sleeping policemen – cruising round wherever the whim or the roadworks take him, kings of the Colosseum like Ben Hur and Stephen Boyd. Britain's going car crazy and as I've explained elsewhere (see page 100), with no prospect of buying cheap from Eastern Europe the punter on a budget is going to be looking at the Previously Owned – or as we in the trade know it, the Classic Car – market. Yet in a future filled with cars, speed will not be of the essence. Luxury and reliability will be tantamount. The demand from all quarters will be such that a lot will be asked of vintage car dealers like my good self and WE WILL NOT LET THE COUNTRY DOWN.

Whether it's a 1960s Vauxhall Viva or a classic Austin Allegro Vanden Plas you're after you need look no further ... every one of them so environmentally conscious that they refuse to go more than thirty miles an hour. In other words, I've got the motors to make you feel you're living in Victorian England again!

THE CHURCH
Take Two Tablets Daley

Make no mistake, the Church is in a right cods. Not since Lindsifarne got a torching from Kirk Douglas and Tony Curtis and them other Vikings has there been so much strife. You've got lemon curds in cassocks – where next, the Directors' Box at Wimbledon Dogs? – Sunday trading and the Archbish of Canterbury having a go at the Government. Who'd have thought it would come to this?

When the Venerable Bede saw the back of those hairy Norwegians, rowing back to Oslo in their funny hats, paid off with an annual retainer and on a promise that they could beat us at football whenever they liked, the way was clear for unfettered Christianity to let rip up and down the land. Although Scotland as usual took a while to get the hang of the what's-mine-is-yours end of things. Churches were put up and apart from a bit of a dust-up between King Harry and Sir Thomas a'Becket one night over five rounds down the Old Kent Road, the Cape of Good Hope was well pleased with the result. His UK branch was generating a nice little bit of turnover, what with each confession costing two and six just to get in the box, and the local priest creaming half your wages for a really bad sin like not eating haddock on Friday. This disposable income was converted by the Pope and his men into art. In fact so much did they treasure their collections and being a bit streetwise they had the oils slapped on the walls and ceilings so that when their paintings became masterpieces no one could half-inch them.

So committed to the Christian cause is our King Richard the Lionheart that he leads a European peacekeeping force to the Middle East to convert all the heathens to the one true faith (a bit like Chelsea fans in the 1970s, sprucing up the Parthenon and other dusty monuments with a nice splash of blue spray-paint) and set up shop in Jerusalem. All he got for his trouble was an arrow somewhere nasty – France, I think – and his kid brother John putting up the taxes. Mind you at least Dick got stuck in like a true Pomegranete, which is a bit more than you can say for the current tenants of Buck House who only get stuck into Caribbean cruises, après ski and the totaliser at Kempton Park.

But then a spanner is well and truly shoved in the works when Henry VIII decides he wants a divorce from one of his many spouses or spice, to give it the correct collective terminology. He was like a medieval Liz Taylor, in more ways than one, and being a bit of a pie-eater he'd begun to get sick of paella, not to mention his Spanish trouble prattling on in her own lingo. The marriage had been cooked up by the politicians but it made nobody at all happy and was regarded very much as the *Eldorado* of its day. So when the Pope cuts up rough about the divorce (he was a single geezer, as they all have been since Pope Joan and even she had a moustache) Henry decides to go it alone and open his own Church. A few compulsory purchases later and he's set for life. The Holy Father, Don Vito Borgia or some such, was an early day Mafia *capo di tutti monte*, and takes all this very personally indeed, which is why a few years down the road when Good Queen Bess was on the hot seat he got Spanish Phil to send the toreadors over (see page 12) to find out how that one worked out).

Anyway, after the Armada had been given the red card it was plain sailing (unlike now when we'd have to derail a couple of trains in the Channel Tunnel, being as how the Navy's down to the Royal Yacht and even that's inked in to be a theme park cruiser moored off Tower Bridge). For four hundred years or more the C of E offered nice employment prospects at home or abroad with steady wages and a roof over your head. If your flesh and blood wasn't quite up to running the family estate or becoming a brief and didn't fancy donning the bearskin and sticking his bayonet up Johnny Gurkha, then taking the cloth was the ideal alternative. Send the fool of the family into the church was the motto: a couple of tombolas, a bit of Christmas cheer and he was in clover.

But how it has all changed. These days your average parish St Whatsits is like Aintree racecourse – deserted for ninety per cent of the time then chocker for a few weeks in spring as young lovers get spliced before the start of the new tax year. The merry organ's got gangrene, the sweet singing in the choir's on cassette and the verger's hang-gliding off the steeple to raise money for a few new slates. Meanwhile the vicar's got a beard and walks round in scruffy trainers (you can't tell 'em apart from London Transport bus conductors), whingeing on about how poor and sick everybody is. In my churchgoing days – we're going back a bit now, but I wasn't going to miss out on the chance of some Maundy Money – his missus would be making an oildrum-load of damson jam and organising a raffle to raise morale. Nowadays *she's* as likely to be the one in the dog collar while he slaves over the Baby Belling.

No wonder nobody drops in at the House of God any more. It's too depressing. Most people find it hard enough getting through the omnibus edition of *EastEnders* on a Sunday afternoon, without being haringayed all morning about the needy. To get people flocking back to church you've got to make it enjoyable. Not to mention warm. As it happens, I know just the sermon that will call out to them.

Now, you're probably wondering just how it is that I am putting my good self forward as the saviour of the Church. Well just like my namesake King Arthur, who sent his Minders of the Round Table out with instructions not to come back without the Holy Grail or there'd be no swan and chips, I too hear a calling. Not that I want to be vaingloriously remembered – I harbour no illusions about becoming Saint Arthur of Fulham, though the Freedom of the Borough wouldn't go amiss, nor its attendant perks. No, I just want to Do My Bit, to strike my own match and hold it up into the light at the end of the tunnel that it may shine brighter for all to see the path of righteousness. You with me?

The first Commandment for getting punters' bums on pews is Incentivisation. When I want the Great British Public to purchase one of my motors you don't hear me saying, 'Come on down to Arthur Daley's – I've got a load of dodgy jam jars to flog'. So it stands to reason that your parish priest has got to excite people's interest, make 'em think they're going to get a result, which is of course where – with my years of successful selling behind me – I step modestly down the aisle, just like I did all that time ago with 'er indoors in those happy loving days before she discovered she wasn't up the duff.

Forget 'It Is Time To See The Lord' and all those pony slogans they stick on their day-glo signs! How about:

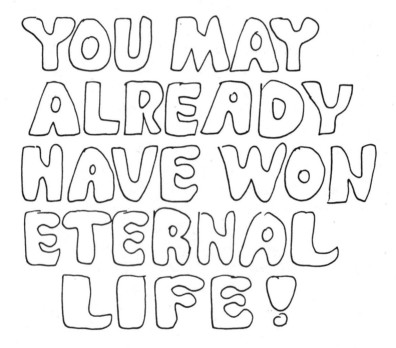

YOU MAY ALREADY HAVE WON ETERNAL LIFE!

Or if they really want to pack 'em in:

IF YOU'RE
THE 99TH
SOUL TO
TAKE
COMMUNION
TODAY
YOU WIN
A TRIP TO
LORD'S!

Forgive me Father, but you've got to market yourself, give the parishioners a reason to sing 'O Come All ye Faithful'.

The next step has to be minimising costs. When Jesus told St Peter to go forth and build his church I don't think he meant put up thirty-seven in Fulham alone. Everyone from soup to nuts, Catholics to Seventh Day Adventists, have got their own gaff. But with an eagle eye on the digital display and a little military precision you could have all the services in one church. Take a leaf out of the Odeon's book: they show Indian films on Sunday mornings and cater for the black-belt and raincoat brethren in all-nighters. There again, if everybody banded together and raised the necessaries you could build a religious Worshiplex with five churches under one roof! That way your punter has customer's choice: whether to go to matins or benediction, have a confession or drop in for a natter with the Lutherans.

Of course I remain a firm believer in tradition when it comes to keeping Sunday special: I'm always out of the Winchester by one o'clock for a spot of 'er indoors's roast pork and crackling. As Pat Boone once said, it's harder for Speedy Gonzales to go to heaven on a camel than it is for a rich man to pass through the eye of a needle. Therefore I cannot tell you how appalled I am by the thought of those High Street giants opening up on the Lord's Day of Rest.

What's going to happen to the small trader already harried by St Michael and Lord Sainsbury? And more important still, what is going to happen to his supplier? The owner of your corner shop doesn't always have time to fill his minivan fit to bursting down Makro with toilet rolls and bakewell tarts. There are times when he is in sore need of the acute merchandising nous of his friendly local wholesaler with a lock-up on site and a boy willing to stack the shelves. One of the most heartwarming developments in racial harmony in recent years has been the rise of the shopkeeper from the Indian and Pakistani subcontinents, and his trusting and as like as not smiling willingness to stock batteries with German instructions, own-brand colas and home improvers from the famous Ronco range.

Returning to my mutton, this aforementioned wholesaler could be the same port of call for the enterprising vicar with an eye for a good line: weeping Virgin Mary lampstands, 'I Don't Believe It!' Bishop of Durham T-shirts, genuine York Minster firelighters, Vatican snowstorms, battery-operated toy Popemobiles (emerges and kisses tarmac), several gross of 'Perry Coma's Fireside Carols' ... the merchandising possibilities are legionary. As someone who has watched the ebb and flow of many a business transaction I can tell you there is no end of fascinating flotsam washed up when the tide goes

Synchronising opening hours with chucking-out time at the local Church of Nostradamus. They're suckers for buying anything marked 'Down In Price While World Lasts'.

out, just sitting there waiting for the right tide to come back in again.

So you see, if you have a little faith every cloud can have a silver lining, with citizens like myself on tap, willing to donate knowledge of their Special Subject – asking in return nothing more than a firm sale. The aisles of our churches just like those of our corner-shops can be filled once again with happy smiling faces on the Sabbath. I like to think a certain Someone who overturned market-stalls in the temple would think twice next time!

THE NEW TECHNOLOGY
Hello Mr Chips

In other chapters of this book it has been a challenge to eradicate the future from the present, but not one beyond a man like myself steeped in the culture and learning of our great nation. But here in the vista of New Technology we are bang up against the $64,000 question with every Tom, Dick and Harry, not to mention Dave, looking for a tip. It's chaos, the boffins in white coats say. A butterfly flaps its wings in Tokyo and the whole of the Home Counties sneezes. No one can predict the future without looking like a global village idiot.

But that is where they are wrong. Look hard enough at the past, Grasshopper, and you will find the seeds that become tomorrow's mighty acorns. Take videos. When the first Betamaxes came on the market you'd be hard pushed fitting more than a gross in the back of a Transit and I got no amount of verbals from my boy, whose job it was to dispatch said appliances to their happy owners, under cover of darkness. Now you could get the lot into two Tesco carrier bags, or matching hand luggage as they call it down Parson's Green.

Colour tellies. You always used to be able to spot the first punter in your street to get one: he had to build an extension on his gaff to fit it in. Now you can stick one in your pocket and watch it when you like – driving, anything. Same with phones. In the Dark Ages businessmen at the cutting edge like myself sometimes failed to clinch a deal because of a wonky florin. Now I can get on the mobile dog. Hi-tech communications networks is what keeps the sharp-witted entrepreneur in the fast lane of the Information Superhighway, with not a cone in sight. With your Cellnet in one hand and Watchman in the other you can be in any situation and still have time to check out the ponies in the paddock before belling Barry the Book to make your wager.

'Course, there is a down side to any technological advance. The video-phone is a definite step backwards. The thought of 'er indoors's boat looming out of some screen at me when I'm down the Winchester hardly bears thinking about. But by and large things have come on since Sir Clive Sinclair hit the ground pedalling in his C5. And the word is that him and Alan Sugar are putting their heads together to develop a system that will rival anything they can come up with in the land of Karaoke – East of Java, where your hardworked executive pushes a button and his home computer runs his bath, cooks his sushi and pours him a stiff SAT (saké-and-tonic).

I of course will be in the van of these developments, with the engine running. Arthur Daley plc is poised to put so much computing power into the British front room that NASA's command centre will look like a branch of Currys after a clearance sale. But you're saying how will I get the hang of it? By following my usual methods – keeping my ear in an interface situation with the ground. In this way I have come to a deep understanding of all the current jargon, a glossary of same I am willing to pass on to you *arts gratis*:

COMPUTER: Looks like a telly and does all sorts of business, depending on your software.

SOFTWARE: Bung it in and it does all sorts of things, e.g. Daley Accounts (TM), an easy step-by-step guide to Home Accounting for the Self-Employed. It takes all the Taxation out of Tax!

WINDOWS: Glass things you look through. Those of us completely oh fay with computers call them 'screens'.

SCREEN: See above.

COMPACT DISC (CD): Very nifty method for record companies to make a bit of bunce. Usually spelt 'Disk' so you don't think you're buying an EP.

CD ROM: Prototype Roman version of the above – suffered because they didn't have any CD players.

CD I: More sophisticated version of above – like motors e.g. SRI, GTI, etc.

VR: Or Virtual Reality – how Dave drifts from day to day. You put some hi-tech bins on and create your own world – England beating the West Indies, sunshine in summer, parking spaces, a business environment free from the petty bureaucracy of meddlesome officials, polite and helpful plod, cheap sherbets. About to be made illegal.

FIBRE OPTICS: Not to be confused with Optic Fibres, the pieces of thread Dave uses at the Winchester when he goes down the cellar, to stop the clientele nipping behind the counter for an illicit gargle. This is the most exciting development of the lot, which means you'll soon be able to shop from the comfort of your own Parker Knoll. Just pick your choice of goods from the telly and then tell it what you want down a dedicated line that goes right to the heart of the warehouse. Imagine – if you will – the citizenry of Fulham exposed to the Aladdin's Cave of Daley Home Shopping. A wide range of desirable consumer durables could be theirs at the push of a button, sending their orders straight to the lock-up from where my boy would speed to the home of the lucky punter with their wise purchases before they'd even drawn breath and contemplated what they'd done. And if he wasn't there inside a half-hour my famous pizza penalty clause would be triggered off, whereby the customer would get the offer of Daley Life Insurance at competitive rates.

Once again I have taken a butcher's into the future, and it works. For yours truly.

CONCLUSIONS

I can hold my hand up and say this about the foregoing pages that have absorbed you over the last few festive days (unless you're still the speed-reading cheapskate mentioned on page 2, go on get back out into the wet!): unlike every other election manifesto that comes thudding through your door along with the cheap pizza offers and the half-price carpet-cleaning deals (it's all the same company, which tells you something about their delivery boys) – every word from the Arthur Daley pen is the honest truth, there isn't a porky within a mile of my bureau.

My humble intention has been to point out the way ahead into the 21st century AD (as it's flatteringly called) while building on the great traditions of this Island Race, and to try and ensure it isn't tainted by such misbegotted ventures as the Channel Tunnel, probably the biggest commercial mistake since the Spirograph (as two back rooms of my lock-up will testify) which will change the lives of such doubty yeoman stock as Dave forever, and not for the better: what'll it mean to a decent mark-up if oceans of cheap Chateau Collapso can come flooding into the country on every luggage-rack?

But mine isn't purely a selfish mission: I recognise that the 1980s are now but a happy memory like the first flush of a honeymoon (or so I'm told) and that perforce the pendulum has swung and we are well into the Caring 90s and already halfway to the 00s. However bitter a pill it has been to swallow, I have to concede that Maggie was wrong about one thing (two if you count allowing John Major to be released into the community): there *is* such a thing as society, and it ain't just the building variety.

Accordingly I have realised it's time to get the old social conscience out from under the stairs, and after soaking it in vinegar overnight it's firing on all cylinders again. Visitors to my forecourt en route via special tour bus from Madame Tussauds to the London Dungeon will note that I am now devoting part of my sales area to Single Parent Family Saloons.

And that's not all. In spite of being the same age as Paul Newman (we have other things in common too and I don't mean the spaghetti hoops sauce), I am a positive Chernobill of energy, diamond schemes tumbling from the Daley bonce and falling into my laptop. If there is one message crying out to the powers-that-be from this book it is this: No fear, Arthur's here – ready, willing and able to contract out his grey cells in the national interest.

I mean, take the 2004 Olympics. At my time of

writing we're *still* trying to stick them where the sun never shines, i.e. Manchester. I ask you – the only place where if the athletes failed a drug test they'd give 'em some! Yet here's Battersea Power Station festering across the water, itching to have itself converted into an Olympic stadium, complete with unrivalled communications to the West End which can be laid on at the drop of a trilby, not to mention a patriotically reduced rate.

Failing that, I am drawing up contingency plans to take Battersea off the scrapheap and put it back to work as Daley World, the ultimate theme park staffed by fresh-faced redcoats plucked from the Old King Cole and operating super-duper rides never seen before by the excited punter, except at Euro-Disney which by then will have turned up its toes.

You see? All this country needs is the right kind of enterprising know-how, combined with a good kick up the jacksie (I haven't even mentioned videos in the backs of people's hats waiting in bus queues). I rest my case, cork up my pen, lay down my mouse. The currant bun's over the yardarm and I reckon I've earned a heart-starting VAT.

You know where to find me.